Again the guard ducked in and slapped at the ball. It bounced off the side of Ben's leg and rolled out-of-bounds. Without thinking, Ben shoved the pesky opponent hard with the heel of his hand. "Get out of my face, shrimp!" he said.

A blast from a whistle pierced the gymnasium. The official ran towards Ben. "Technical foul! If I see that again, son, you're out of the game."

No one needed to tell Ben that he had just made a fool of himself. By the time he reached his chair he was so frustrated and angry at everyone, including himself, that he wanted to cry.

Full Court Press

NATE AASENG

Chariot Books™
David C. Cook Publishing Co.

To the memory of my grandfathers

A White Horse Book
Published by Chariot Books™,
an imprint of David C. Cook Publishing Co.
David C. Cook Publishing Co., Elgin, Illinois 60120
David C. Cook Publishing Co., Weston, Ontario

FULL COURT PRESS
© 1990 by Nathan Aaseng

Cover design by Loran Berg
Cover illustration by Paul Turnbaugh
First printing, 1990
Printed in the United States of America
94 93 92 91 90   5 4 3 2 1

Library of Congress Cataloging-in-Publication Data

Aaseng, Nathan.
  Full court press/Nate Aaseng.
    p. cm.
  Summary: When Ben, the star of his church basketball team,
finds himself turning into a poor sport and a ball hog, he receives
spiritual support through anonymous notes from a secret admirer.
  ISBN 1-55513-821-7
  [1. Basketball—Fiction. 2. Conduct of life—Fiction.]
I. Title.
PZ7.A13Fu 1990
[Fic]—dc20   90-34474
                                                           CIP
                                                           AC

Contents

1 The Toe 7
2 Homework 14
3 The Mystery Note 23
4 The Shot 32
5 A Suspect 46
6 Miscalculation 54
7 Good Shots 62
8 The Lay-up 76
9 Technical Foul 84
10 Night of Terror 96
11 Grandpa 109
12 Brook Manor Mavericks 120
13 The Last Shot 130

1
The Toe

"Do you suppose I could find an incredibly strong kid somewhere to help me haul these things?"

Benjamin Oakland continued to dribble with his left hand as he turned to look at his father who was holding a square slab of concrete. Ben could see a stack of similar slabs weighing down the trunk of their car.

"Sure, Dad." The boy flicked one more shot at the basket. When it clanged off the rim, he retrieved it and shot once more from in close. Ben's hands were growing cold. A November breeze chased away any warmth that the sun might have given, so he had little control of the ball. Again the shot missed its mark. Frowning, he attempted one more lay-up. This one was successful.

Despite the brisk weather, Ben's short brown hair was matted with sweat. Except for slightly hollow cheeks and eyebrows that tufted at the peaks, he was a very average-looking boy.

After tossing his basketball in a cardboard box in

the garage, he peered into the open trunk.

"Be careful with those—they're heavy," said Dad, his hands grimy from preparing the ground for the blocks. "Just bring a couple of them out back."

Ben hoisted one and grunted at how heavy it was. "Where's Ken?" he asked. Whenever there was work to be done and Ben was doing it, his first thoughts turned to his older brother. In the Oakland family, the older you were, the more slave labor was expected of you. Ben wanted to make sure the oldest slave was not getting away with anything.

"He's coming," said Dad as he hauled his load through the back door of the garage.

Reinforcements quickly arrived, but not the kind Ben was looking for. "Can we help?" asked little sister April, bouncing across the garage floor. Apparently she included Nick, the youngest of the Oaklands, in the offer.

"Look out. This is too heavy for you," Ben said. "Stay out of my way." The rough corners of the concrete were biting into his already stiff fingers, and Ben was glad when he reached the backyard and set down his load.

"I've got some gloves you can use," Dad said, seeing Ben wring his hands. "Just bring a couple more of those. Ken can handle the rest."

"Nah, I'll be all right once I get these gloves on." Although not particularly fond of work, Ben was not about to back down from the chance to show he was at least as tough as Ken.

"Get out of the way, please," he said, irritated, as Nick and April tried to help him carry the next load. "It's too heavy for you. Why don't you go find that lazy Ken and tell him to get down here." April scampered away, eager to deliver the message, with Nick trailing.

By the time Ken arrived, Ben was on his fourth slab. Although his arms were beginning to shake from the exertion, Ben pretended to be okay.

"Why don't you take a break—this isn't a fire drill," Dad said.

"I can get another one unloaded first," Ben said. This time, though, he could feel the strain all the way through to the sockets of his shoulders. He took shorter, more hurried steps toward the door. But there was Nick, blocking the exit with his wagon. "Come on, you guys are making it twice the work! Get of of here!" Ben grunted.

By the time he squeezed past Nick, Ben felt his grip beginning to slip. He lurched out the door but before he could set the block down, he caught his foot on a roll of sod that Dad had pulled up to make room for the blocks. Ben stumbled, and the concrete ripped off one of his gloves as it slid out of his grasp. The edge of the concrete block landed with crushing force squarely on Ben's big toe.

Ben's screams were enough to summon Mom from the basement. Bare arms crossed to ward off the outdoor climate, she pushed her way past the curious brothers and sister. Dad was doing his best to calm Ben who was still hopping around on one foot and yelling.

"Tom, what was he doing carrying those heavy blocks?" scolded Mom.

"He thought it was a basketball and he dribbled it off his foot," said Ken.

"This is not a time for cute remarks," Mom said, angrily.

"They weren't heavy!" Ben answered through clenched teeth and tears that were beginning to spill from his blue eyes. "I tripped on that sod. Oh, ow!"

"I'm sorry. I shouldn't have left that sod there. I thought there was enough room to get through," said Dad. "Can you settle down enough so we can have a look at it?"

When Ben finally submitted to an examination, the Oaklands peeled off a blood-stained sock to find an ugly, swollen mess.

"Whew!" whistled Ken. "Looks like you really nailed it."

"Does it hurt?" asked April.

"No, it tickles!"

"We'd better have a doctor look at it," Dad said. He searched the pockets of his baggy garden clothes, then got up and hurried inside the house.

Nick kept complaining that he couldn't see, so Ken picked him up and held him over the wound. "If you were a horse we'd probably have to shoot you," Ken said to Ben. "Isn't that the pits, though? The only three things you've talked about for the last five months are basketball, basketball, and basketball. Now here it is, less than two weeks before the season starts, and you get yourself so mashed up that you'll have to sit out a couple of months."

Until that moment the searing pain had blocked out all other thoughts and feelings. But it was as if Ken's words struck a nerve even more sensitive than those in his feet. All of a sudden Ben shrieked and slammed his fist into the lawn.

"What did you do now?" Dad asked, coming out of the house.

"I didn't touch him," Ken said, putting Nick down. "I just said it was too bad he was going to be laid up for the start of basketball practice."

"Why couldn't you just carry your own stupid blocks?! Idiotic sod! You can just take your whole patio and . . ."

Mom's eyes flashed alarm as Ben continued to beat the earth. "Benjamin, calm down. That's just going to make it worse. Try to relax, would you?"

"I can't figure out what I did with the car keys," Dad said, his jaw clenched in frustration.

"I know! They're still in the trunk. I saw them there!" said April, proudly.

When Dad and Ben finally got in the car, and those begging to come along had been shooed away, Dad tried reassuring Ben that it might not be as bad as he thought. "Sometimes these things look worse than they really are. And even if you have to sit on the sidelines awhile, it might not be all bad. You'll be raring to go just about the time everyone else is getting a little tired of the game—you'll give the whole team a lift."

Ben didn't answer. For one thing, the toe still throbbed so badly he thought it might explode. For another, he could not imagine anyone getting tired of playing basketball. But the most important reason was that November 8 had been circled in purple marker on his calendar since early last spring. It had been tough counting down the days until that first practice.

If there was one thing Ben was no good at, it was waiting. As soon as he became aware of some future event, it was as if someone planted a noisy clock in the center of his brain. No matter how he tried, he could not stop thinking about it until it nearly drove him crazy. Now, just as he was nearing the end of the wait—this!

Slumped back in the rear seat, resting his leg on the seat, Ben brooded about the injustice of it all. There he was being a good kid, helping his parents, working hard and not even complaining. And what was his reward?

A half hour later, Dr. Weber filled him in on the details of his "reward." It was more like a prison term. Ben had been sentenced to at least two weeks of no activity, and then at least two more of light activity, which meant something other than basketball. After that, Dr. Weber would check to see how he was doing. Then, just *maybe*, he would give the okay.

As they were leaving the doctor's office, Dad tried to cheer Ben up. "It turned out better than I thought," he said. "You just clipped the fat part of your toe. When I first pulled off your sock, I thought you might have broken the thing in a dozen places."

But Ben wasn't listening. "Dr. Weber didn't say that I couldn't shoot baskets, did he?" he asked, hobbling through the parking lot on crutches. "That isn't really any kind of activity. I mean, I can shoot baskets standing still."

2
Homework

Whether or not Dr. Weber approved of Ben shooting baskets, Mom made it clear what she thought of the idea. "No activity means *no activity*, young man." He could not even bounce a basketball sitting in a basement chair without the little kids complaining about the noise.

"Come on! They can hear the TV. They're just being twerps, as usual," he grumbled. He expected his sore foot to win him some sympathy but Mom seemed to be going out of her way to make him miserable. Ben could have sworn she was glad he smashed his toe, just to keep him away from the thing he loved most in life. She insisted there would be no bouncing basketballs in the house, even in the basement. Ben couldn't even win that one.

Resenting his family's lack of understanding and frustrated by the slow healing of his toe, Ben could hardly stand to be around the house. For the first time in his life he was actually glad for the end of the long Thanksgiving weekend so he could get back to school and be with normal people. By that time he could have done without the crutches, but he liked to use them anyway. As long as he had to have an injury, he might as well look like a real injured basketball player!

After supper on the Tuesday after Thanksgiving, Ben went out into the darkness, clomping his way down the street to their church. The River Metro basketball league included both school and church teams. This fact had caused Ben a great deal of anguish during the early days of November. Everyone knew how good Ben Oakland was and they had all been begging him to join their team. Ben took it for granted that Pine Knoll School would have a better team than Faith Church. In fact, if he joined the Pine Knoll team they would easily be the best in the league. Pine Knoll also had a better coach—one of the school gym teachers. Faith had John Buckwell's dad for a coach. You could never tell how much dads knew about a sport—sometimes they just coached as a favor to their own kids.

But when Paul Schmidt and Dave Yamagita joined the church team, Ben decided to go along with them. When it came right down to it, he could not walk out on his closest friends. *Pablo and Rags owe me one for this,* he thought, using their pet names for each other. Ben's nickname was "Oak."

Ben maneuvered his way inside the door of the church gymnasium. Already there were echoing volleys of basketballs bouncing off the floor. This

15

was the Faith Falcons' third practice. Despite the fact that it was sheer torture watching everyone else shoot, Ben could not stay away. At least here he could hold and bounce a basketball without getting chewed out. Every once in a while, when Coach Buckwell's back was turned, he even put up a shot.

"Hi, legless," greeted Pablo.

"Hi, brainless," Ben answered with a smile. They got no further into conversation before Coach Buckwell blew the whistle and gathered the troops under one basket. Ben scooped up a basketball, rubbed his hand over the worn, pebbled surface, and sat down next to the door.

The coach started them off with a lay-up drill. A few lay-ups told you all you needed to know about a person's basketball skill, Ben decided. You could tell that Rags had played before. He took his two steps and gently one-handed the ball up to the backboard. Although he didn't always make the shot, he knew what he was doing. Too bad he was so short. Pablo was an in-betweener. Big boned and solidly built, he relied much more on strength than grace. He sometimes took too many steps and often bounced the ball too hard off the backboard. But at least he had the general idea.

Then there were the Austin Lunds of the world. Austin could not run and dribble at the same time. His imitation of a lay-up was to clumsily bounce the ball two dozen times as he made his way toward the basket, then stop and shoot with two hands from

16

underneath. Austin was not the only one who played like that, but he stood out from the others for a very good reason: Austin Lund was the tallest kid that Ben had ever seen. At six feet, one and a half inches, he even looked down on Coach Buckwell.

Austin did not go to Pine Knoll School, and Ben had never been in the same Sunday school class with him at Faith. The few times he had seen him around the church, he assumed that Austin was three or four years older. So when he saw Austin at the Falcons' first practice, Ben got excited. What an advantage to have someone that big playing under the basket!

That excitement, however, had lasted only as long as it took for Austin to "jump" for a rebound in the Falcons' first practice. Ben was not sure Austin's feet ever left the ground. It didn't matter much though, because the ball went through Austin's hands and hit him in the face. Ben had never before considered basketball a dangerous game. But as Austin sat on the sidelines holding a tissue to his rather large nose, Ben got the feeling that any time there was a ball in flight, the poor guy was not safe.

On this evening, Austin managed to avoid any embarrassing collisions with the ball. But that was the best that could be said for him. Coach Buckwell was trying to practice a full court press on defense. It seemed a good idea to have four players taking chances and swarming all over the dribbler while the giant waited under the basket as the last line of defense. Unfortunately, the last line of defense might as well have been made of air for all the good Austin was doing. The poor guy never met a fake that he didn't fall for. Pablo gave him the same fake three different times, and Austin went for it every time. As for shooting free throws, Austin was doing well if he hit the rim. One of his shots went *over* the backboard.

"At least he must be stronger than he looks," Ben commented later. "He's so skinny I didn't think he could throw a ball that far."

"Austin may be a giant, but I don't think he's going to do us any good," Pablo said afterwards. As the next largest player on the team, Pablo would probably end up playing center. He did not look forward to trying to shoot over kids who were four inches taller.

"This stuff's all new to him," Rags said.

"Yeah," Ben agreed. "I wonder what planet he's been living on. I can't imagine how someone that tall managed to avoid basketball for so long. Maybe if we work with him, he'll start to catch on. It would be a shame to let all that height go to waste."

"You know what will happen?" Rags sniffed. "He'll be the one who ends up making a million dollars playing pro basketball just because he's 7 feet tall."

"Well right now it doesn't matter how short you are," Ben comforted him. "If you played one-on-one with him, you could beat him blindfolded."

That night, Ben leaned back in his chair and wadded up a small piece of paper. "Lakers lead by four, with three minutes to go," he imagined. "The pass goes in to Ben Oakland. Magic Johnson is all over him. Here comes James Worthy on the trap. Oakland fakes a pass and cuts right through the double-team. He goes up." Ben fired the paper ball toward the wastebasket next to his bed. The wad bounced off the bedspread and into the basket. "He's hacked on the arm by Johnson but the shot goes in anyway. Oakland steps to the foul line with a chance for a three-point play."

Just then the door opened. Dad poked his head in and immediately saw the pile of spitballs lying beside the wastebasket. His dark eyebrows raised in suspicion. "Got your homework done?"

Ben straightened his chair and glanced at the open pages of his math book. "Just about."

Dad walked in and bent over Ben, one calloused hand leaning on the desk. "Suppose you show me what 'just about' means."

"Oh, I just have a few problems left on this page." Ben took up his pencil and began studying the next problem.

"How many?"

"Just five or six," Ben sighed, sounding exasperated. "It won't take me that long."

"Uh-huh. You've been sitting up here for more than an hour. And how many problems have you done in that time? Don't answer, I can see only two

19

on your paper. Two down, six to go and you call this 'almost done'?"

"I don't get it, though," whined Ben. "This stuff's too hard."

"How would you know?" asked Dad. "I see you've spent the whole time taking target practice. Do you know what time it is?"

Ben glanced at his digital clock. "About 10 o'clock."

"Nearly quarter *past* 10 o'clock!" Dad said sternly. "You've got 20 minutes to work on your math. After that it's lights out. Whatever isn't done, isn't done and you can either get up early and do it or explain to your teacher why it isn't done. Understand?"

Ben did not answer. He hated math and he hated getting chewed out. It was all Dad's fault anyway. If he hadn't made him carry those blocks and left the sod right in the middle of the doorway, Ben wouldn't be missing so much basketball. If he could just play a little basketball every day, maybe he wouldn't be so bored. Then he would be able to get his math done. But no, he just had to sit and watch without even bouncing a basketball, thanks to Mom. They didn't even try to understand. They just liked bossing people around.

"How come I'm the only one who ever has homework?" Ben grumbled, poking the lead of his pencil through a hole in his sweatpants. "Ken's just sitting downstairs watching TV."

"That's because he sat down and did his home-work instead of filling up wastebaskets with tiny packages. Now I mean it, 20 minutes!"

Twenty minutes later, the door burst open. Ben slammed shut the basketball magazine that he had been reading and spread his math paper over the top of it. Desperately, he hoped it was Ken coming to bed. But he could sense immediately by the size of the shadow that it was Dad again.

Without a word, Dad crossed the floor and snatched Ben's paper. It was virtually unchanged from the last time he had seen it. A second later he unearthed the *Pro Basketball* magazine. Dad did not get *really* angry often but Ben knew this would be one of those times. Ben was caught totally de-fenseless—he could not think of a single ex-cuse—and he sat there almost in shock at his own stupidity.

"That does it!" Dad said, biting off each word. "I gave you 20 minutes to work on your assignment and you thought it would be cute to ignore me and read a basketball magazine. You're grounded for the week, and that includes basketball practice."

"No!" Ben said defiantly. His embarrassment had turned to anger on hearing the punishment. Why did they always pick on basketball? It was the one thing in the whole world that he really cared about. He'd already been cut off from it, and they still could not leave it alone. "You can make me go to bed earlier or fine me or make me do dishes for a week but you can't keep me out of basketball!"

"Don't tell me what I can and can't do! You're not setting the rules here! Furthermore you are not going to any basketball practices, healthy or not, unless you have every assignment finished by 9 o'clock in the evening every single school night of the year. Do you understand me?"

There it was again! Always out to get basketball! First Mom and now Dad. A pair of tag team wrestlers. They find the spot where they can hurt you the most and then take turns stomping on it until you give up. It was just mean and spiteful. "I'm not missing any basketball," he insisted, coldly.

"That's up to you," said Dad. "But what I said stands. If basketball is getting in the way of the important things you have to do, then you'll have to learn to do without it. Now can I trust you to get to bed or do I have to stand here and watch you do it?"

When Ken came to bed a few minutes later, Ben pretended to be asleep. He was finished with trying to be reasonable with people in this family.

3
The Mystery Note

The Oakland family penitentiary was at least bearable during December. Ben had to respect the threat of losing out on basketball, so he always finished his assignments by the appointed time. He also knew better than to bring on more arguments by being openly rude or by being too silent. Since he wanted as little to do with his family as possible, he decided it was best to meet the minimum standards of behavior. He would not be unpleasant but he would not be pleasant, either. He would answer questions but he would not volunteer any information. Even April and Nick got the cool treatment. Maybe they were just little kids, but they were part of the whole situation.

The day finally came, a week later than promised, when Ben was given permission to play some basketball. The toe still had to be heavily wrapped, and Ben was forbidden to take part in competition until after New Year's Day. That meant that he would miss the first two games, which were scheduled for the week after Christmas. But at least he could practice.

Even though a dusting of snow was swirling in the driveway under thick clouds, Ben ran outside with his basketball. Never mind that the ball lost some of its bounce in the cold weather, and that the thick gloves hampered his shooting. This was basketball, and there could be no Christmas present that would equal the thrill of watching that first shot swish through the net.

At Tuesday night practice, Ben felt as though he could soar higher and run faster than anyone else. There was no place on earth he would rather be than on a basketball floor, and it was not costing him a cent to be there!

Coach Buckwell dampened some of the fun by enforcing the doctor's ban on all competitive drills. "The more careful you are in this sport, the more you get stepped on, it seems," Coach told him. "For now, just join in the shooting and passing drills and hold off on the scrimmages. Listen up, everybody!" he called, in his gravelly voice. "Listen up. I want you all to pair off and just practice passing and catching. Mix in some bounce passes."

Pablo whistled at Ben to join him, but Ben shook his head. He had been fascinated by something he had read in a sports article about how the true measure of a great player is that he can make everyone around him play better. Ben decided that if he wanted to be great, he would have to work on doing that. What better person to practice on than Austin Lund? As tall as he was, if someone could teach him to play ball, he could make the Falcons one tough team.

"Go ahead with Rags," Ben said to Pablo. "I want to get to know our giant a little better. Hey, Austin! Over here."

Austin seemed surprised to have been singled out. As he jogged over, Ben noticed that his small head made him look even taller. Austin was so timid on the court that Ben was surprised at how friendly he was. "So you're Ben. I hear you're pretty good."

Ben grinned. "And you're Austin. I hear you're pretty tall."

Austin shook his head. "Just a vicious rumor. I only look tall because I'm so skinny, and because my head is so high off the ground."

"Have you ever played basketball before?" Ben asked as he tossed him a chest high pass.

Austin's hands gave away the answer before the fellow could open his mouth. He stiffened up as the ball came toward him, as if this were a difficult trick he was being asked to perform. "I've never played any sport before," smiled Austin, after making a bobbling catch.

"How come?" Ben asked, casually latching onto Austin's pass with one hand.

"I never thought I was any good. I know, I know," he laughed. "You can't imagine what ever gave me that idea!"

"So what made you try now?" Ben purposely threw soft passes. This was almost like playing catch with Nick.

"I keep growing and everyone says I should play basketball. You know, if you have webbed feet you're supposed to swim. If you have feathers, you're supposed to fly. If you're tall, you're supposed to play basketball."

"How do you like it so far?" Ben risked a bounce pass to Austin and to his surprise, the guy caught it.

"It isn't so much a matter of liking it as it is just surviving," admitted Austin. "When I come out here I feel like I'm in a foreign country where everyone knows the language but me."

"Well, how smart are you? You know this game is just as much mental as it is being coordinated."

"I'm the most brilliant C student in the whole metro area," smiled Austin. "It's funny. People see how clumsy I am at sports and they automatically think I'm a superbrain."

"Well, it works both ways," Ben said. "People see I can play basketball and they think I'm stupid. Shoot, my parents think I'm stupid *because* I play basketball. But, hey, don't worry about it. Being tall really will make it easier for you. You'll like the game once you get used to it," Ben said. "Here, throw the ball straight out from your chest, not from the side. Keep doing it as hard as you can; don't worry about hurting me."

Austin did as he was told, and Ben actually

thought he could detect some improvement. "Thanks for the help," Austin said when a whistle blast ended the drill. "Most of the others act like I'm some kind of freak."

"Hey, you work hard, you can help this team," shrugged Ben. "Tell you what. I know the janitor at this church pretty well. If you want, we can come over here every afternoon during winter break and I can work with you."

The suggestion seemed to stump Austin. "Well, that's really a nice offer. Maybe I could. You got any tips on playing defense?" Austin changed the subject. "I think it's even more embarrassing having people score against me than it is not being able to score against them."

"Didn't the coach tell you anything?" Ben asked, in a voice low enough so that Coach Buckwell couldn't hear. "The best tip on defense is don't look at the other guy's head or you'll get faked out. Keep your eye on his belly button. There aren't too many guys who can fake with their belly button."

"All right. Except that most kids' belly buttons are quite a ways down there."

Ben romped through the lay-up drills without a miss in six attempts. At the free throw line he sank 6 of 10 shots. That was a little below average for him, but he still tied Rags for the best mark on the team. Austin kept his streak alive by missing all 10 of his. After that, Coach Buckwell put the team through scrimmages. Ben begged one more time to join in,

27

but was waved away. He moved off by himself to the far end of the court to practice dribbling with either hand.

Coach Buckwell was determined to use the full court press on defense. That meant they were to guard the other team closely all over the court and never give them a chance to rest. The only defender who was to fall back on defense was the center. Unfortunately during this evening's practice, the press only worked when Rags was playing defense. Whenever Rags was on offense he just dribbled past the defense as if they were flags on a ski racing course. In the mass of confusion, one of the forwards would always get open under the basket. Rags would simply throw a long pass to Pablo, who would fake out Austin for an easy basket. There was one hopeful moment when Austin actually blocked a shot, but Pablo retrieved the loose ball and laid it in for the score.

"When you get in the lineup we can probably work the press pretty well, Oak," Pablo said to Ben as he and Rags waited for their ride after practice.

"Coach will have to put Pablo in at center, though," Rags said, after checking first to make sure that Austin wasn't around. "Austin just isn't ready for prime time."

"I don't think he ever will be," Pablo said. "He could be the most improved player on the team at the end of the year and still be the worst player in the league."

"Give him time," Ben said. "He's never played before. I predict he'll do some serious damage before the season's over."

"He's already done more damage to his nose than any player I ever saw," said Rags.

"Don't be so hard on him," Ben said. "Have you ever talked to him? He's really kind of funny."

"You mean he talks just like he plays?" chuckled Pablo.

Ben shrugged them off and sat down to put on his boots. Three inches of snow had fallen since school was out, and his mom always had a fit about him getting his "expensive" basketball shoes wet. That was typical, the way she cared more about his shoes than about him.

As Ben slid a foot inside one boot, though, it brushed against a lump. Thinking the liner in the boot had gotten bunched up, Ben stuck his hand in to straighten it. But instead of finding soft fabric, his fingers touched something colder and smoother. It was a bright blue envelope.

"Do you always have mail inside your boots?" laughed Rags.

"What's it say, Oak?" asked Pablo. "Who's it from?"

Ben tore open the unaddressed envelope. Inside was a small sheet of paper with a note. The printing was so childish that Ben could hardly read it. Rags, peering over Ben's shoulder, figured it out before Ben could hide it.

" 'Hope you had a nice practice. We're pulling for you all the way. Signed, Order of the Broken Arrow.' Whoa, pretty heavy stuff!" said Rags. "Oak's got some secret admirers!"

"Did one of you guys stick this in here?" demanded Ben. Both his friends denied any knowledge of it. "So who put it in? Did you see anyone messing with my boots?"

"You had your boots out here in the hall, Oak," said Rags. "It could have been anyone. We never would have seen them."

"This is weird," frowned Ben.

"Aw, enjoy it!" said Rags. "How many guys have their own fan club? I don't know how you do it, you sly fox! Girls are so hot on you they start sending notes. Boy, that's rough."

"What makes you think this is from girls?" Ben asked.

"I'll bet it was the crutches," Pablo said. "I read that girls really go crazy for guys on crutches. I could use some attention like that. Could one of you guys step on my foot, just hard enough so I have an excuse to use them?"

"How about if I step on your face?" Ben shot back. "Maybe the girls will think that's an improvement."

"Here's our ride," said Rags opening the door and letting a cool rush of air inside. "You'll just have to suffer with being popular."

"Can I have your autograph?" Pablo called back

as he followed Rags to the idling car.

"For a dollar," Ben answered. Now that the others were gone, he unfolded the crumpled paper and reread it. This was really strange! In a way it felt good to have someone claiming to be a fan of his. Even though he was too suspicious to trust it completely, just reading the words and pretending gave him a small ego lift.

But Ben had no more patience for mysteries than he had for anything else. The clues kept nagging at him. The babyish writing really had him puzzled. And who or what was the Order of the Broken Arrow? As he walked home he tried to figure out who would do such a thing. But even after running a long list of acquaintances through his mind, Ben could not even come up with one suspect.

4
The Shot

Ben sat glumly on the edge of the stage, wondering why he had bothered to put on his red Falcons uniform. After all, Coach Buckwell had made it clear that Ben would not be playing in this game against the Patterson Panthers.

As he watched the two squads miss shots, kick the ball around, and throw passes out-of-bounds, Ben could hardly believe they had spent a month practicing basketball skills.

"I could score 50 points against these guys," he thought. Having to sit there on the bench watching a game was much harder than watching practice. It was all he could do to keep from running out and grabbing the basketball.

Although this was the first game Ben had seen, it was not the Falcons' first game. They had been manhandled by the Lincoln Bay Lakers 46-10 just two nights earlier. Ben's absence had been the result of more troubles on the home front, on Christmas Day, of all times.

It all started when Nick asked Ben to read the books on dinosaurs he had gotten for Christmas. In the spirit of the season, Ben had turned up his personality a notch on the pleasantness scale, and had already read two books to his younger brother that morning. By the time Nick came begging for a third reading, Ben was busy working on his Boston Celtics team picture jigsaw puzzle, a surprise gift from Mom.

"I'm sorry, Nick, I already read to you twice," he had said. "Now I'm in the middle of something I want to do. Get Ken to read it."

"Ken's helping April with that stupid Magic Dungeon game."

"How about Dad or Grandpa?"

Nick clambored up the stairs only to return to the basement with an irritating news bulletin. "Grandpa's playing with April and Mom says they're busy making dinner and you're not doing anything so you have to read it to me. So there!"

Had he remained calm and taken some time to think about it, Ben might have had realized that Nick was not the most accurate reporter. As a matter of fact, the kid had twisted Ben's statement to Mom as well as Mom's message to Ben. Ben's blue eyes flashed anger, however, and rather than checking out Nick's story, he called off the Christmas truce.

"Sure, I'll read it to you," he said, as Nick climbed on his lap. Flipping quickly through the pages, he

33

read, "Dinosaurs were big creatures. They ate elephants and bananas and slept in abandoned garbage trucks and now they're all dead. The end." With that he slammed the book shut and booted Nick off his lap.

"That's not what it said!" Nick screamed. Seconds later most of Ben's jigsaw puzzle pieces were dashed to the floor and Nick's bottom was swatted as tears and angry shouts drowned out the Christmas music on the stereo. Mom, who had been frantically trying to get a perfect meal together while everything was still hot, blew her top.

Tired of being pushed around, Ben refused to apologize. Despite Dad's and Grandpa's best efforts at peacemaking, the argument grew more heated until Ben stomped off up to his room.

"You're not missing Christmas dinner!" Mom yelled up to him. "If you don't come down right now, you can forget about going to your basketball game tomorrow."

Ben had not come down, and it had been a thoroughly miserable Christmas for everyone, especially with all of it happening in front of Grandpa. Dad backed up the punishment of missing the first game, and so Ben had been spared the agony of watching his team get creamed.

Mom gave up speaking to him after that, and for a time the little kids stared at him as if he were some dangerous criminal. Ken kept telling him he was "immature," and Dad had been surprisingly quiet on the whole subject. The only relief Ben found during the week had been those afternoon practice sessions at the church gym with Austin. The big guy seemed eager to learn and Ben was eager to teach him. They fired passes at the wall from close range and tried to catch them; fortunately the finger Austin sprained was on his left hand. Then they worked on shooting free throws, and shuffling the feet on defense. Ben even taught Austin the hook shot and had him repeat the maneuver again and again.

The second session didn't last as long as the first, and Austin kept glancing at his watch. The big guy didn't always seem to be paying attention to what Ben was saying, especially after the first half hour. But Ben was seeing improvement. If they kept at it every day of vacation, there might be some hope for the new center.

In this game against Patterson, though, Austin Lund was hardly a beacon of hope. After entering the game in the second period, Austin only touched the ball once—when a rebound bounced off his shoulder and into the hands of a Panther. On offense, Rags looked at Austin several times, but always thought better about risking a pass to him. Fortunately, the Patterson guards were having such trouble handling the ball that they never got any fast break chances against Austin.

Just before halftime, though, Austin produced a blunder of such magnificence that even his opponents were wincing in embarrassment for him. The gangly center was knocked over in a scramble after a rebound. A Panther was called for the foul, and that put Austin on the free throw line, all by himself, in front of everybody. As the referee handed him the ball, Austin blinked and gulped and trembled as though he were facing a firing squad.

After bouncing the ball for what seemed like five minutes, he summoned the courage to risk a shot. He bent his knees the way Ben had shown him. But as he let the ball go, he lost his balance and teetered over the foul line. Swinging his arms to regain control, he struggled to keep his feet behind the line as the ball sailed in a high arc toward the hoop. All of his efforts were in vain. He crashed to the floor in the lane without anyone touching him.

Miraculously, the ball went through the net, but that only made matters worse. The referee took away the point because Austin crossed over the foul line. Ben thought it was an act of mercy when Coach Buckwell promptly removed Austin from the game. It was especially thoughtful of Coach to put in three substitutes at once so that Austin would not feel like he was yanked out for sheer clumsiness.

"Doesn't look good for us," said John Buckwell, the coach's son, as he sat down next to Ben. His round face was flushed. John was the heaviest of the Falcon players, and after several minutes of chasing the Panthers around the court, he seemed glad to have a replacement.

"We're only down by four points," shrugged Ben. "The game isn't even half over."

"Yeah, but this is supposed to be the worst team in the league," huffed John as he wiped his forehead with the bottom of his shirt.

The statement jolted Ben out of his slouch. "Where did you hear that?" he asked. Even though Ben had not been involved in the loss to the Lakers, he was ashamed of the score. The thought of adding to that humiliation by losing to the worst team in the league was almost more than he could take.

"They lost by 20 points to the Redeemer Rockets in their first game," John said. "A lot of those Rockets go to my school, and they aren't very good."

Nobody scored in the final two minutes of the period, so the halftime score stood at 13-9 in favor of the Panthers. Rags had scored seven of the Falcons' points and Chris Moret, one of the reserve forwards, had scored the other basket on a rebound. Pablo had tried two shots early in the first quarter and both had been blocked. After that he seemed only too eager to pass the ball.

As the group gathered around Coach Buckwell in one corner of the gym, several of the players were complaining to others about their poor passes. For some reason, it took the Coach a long time to get his thoughts together. Twice he asked for quiet, but each time he got it, he just ran a large hand through his wavy, grayish hair and stared at the floor until the chattering started up again.

"My toe feels great," Ben said. "I got it all taped up just in case. Can't I play, please?"

"You guys want to play?" Coach said. "Then let's have it quiet." Several more seconds went by before he said, "All right. You're doing fine. I see lots of hustle. There's a lot of mistakes but they're hustle mistakes and those will go away once you get some experience. You need to think about what you're doing, now. David, don't start dribbling as soon as you get the ball. When you catch the ball you have two options: you can either pass or dribble. If you start dribbling right away and then have to stop, then your only choice is to pass the ball. That makes it too easy for the defense. Look for the pass first, then dribble."

"Can I play? Just a few minutes," begged Ben. "The toe's perfect and I promise I'll stay out of traffic. I'll just play around the outside."

Coach turned on him slowly, his gray eyes peeking out of his thick eyelids. "Do you understand English? Your doctor said to avoid contact 'til after New Year's. That's final. Now, second half," he started. Obviously Ben had distracted him because he stared at his sheet of paper for several seconds before continuing. "Remember I'm going to give everyone some playing time. We'll keep getting fresh troops in there so we can always play tough, full court defense. Chuck and Nathan at guards to start out with. Chris and John at forward. How's the elbow, Austin? You ready to play?" Austin nodded nervously and Coach finished, "Austin at center."

Ben trudged back to the stage, flanked by Rags and Pablo. "You guys can't let these jokers beat you," Ben said. "We'll never be able to show our faces at school again."

"What do you want from me?" Rags said wearily. "I'm doing everything I can."

Pablo glanced up sheepishly. "I didn't have a very good half. I don't think I was warmed up enough. Maybe it's because I had to sit in the cold car for five minutes before Dad finally got ready." He glanced up at the rows of chairs on the stage to see if his dad was close enough to hear.

Ben thought again about how nice it would have been to have played on the Pine Knoll team. They had some good, tall players like Rudy and Rich. If he were on the Pine Knoll Knicks he wouldn't have to worry about the teasing at school, or about being embarrassed by his own teammates. Except for Rags, the Falcons were too slow. Except for Austin, who hardly counted, they were too short.

Ben was tempted to take a dig at his friends for insisting they play on the church team. But they were discouraged, and you had to give it to poor Rags—he was playing his heart out. Ben refused to lose hope. Things would be different once he got back into action. If only Austin could learn a few of the basics, then Pablo could play forward where he could do a better job, and then they'd do all right.

39

The Falcon unit that Coach Buckwell sent out did nothing to change the team's fortunes. In five minutes they went scoreless, and gave up two baskets to the Panthers.

"Come on, now. It's 17-9. Don't let them get away from you!" Ben shouted as Rags, Pablo, and John ran out onto the court. He could not sit still and began fidgeting on the stairs leading up to the stage. School vacation would soon be over and he knew just what he would hear even before he got his coat off in the classroom. Rudy would be laughing his head off at how the Falcons lost to the crummy Panthers.

Rags was all over the court, his straight black hair whipping from side to side with each screeching halt and change of direction. By the end of the quarter, the team had cut the margin to 18-15, thanks to two steals by Rags in the Panthers' backcourt, and foul shots by Pablo and Nathan.

"You're getting them, now!" Ben said, as the Falcons huddled up before starting the final period. "Keep on them!" He was so pumped up he didn't know what to do with his hands. He kept clenching and unclenching his fists and trying to keep his stomach muscles from tying themselves into knots.

The final quarter was pure agony for Ben. Rags would steal a pass only to slip and lose the ball to the Panthers. Pablo would block a shot only to have the nearsighted referee blow the whistle on him for a foul. Austin would catch a ball under the basket

40

only to have it knocked out of his hands before he could try a shot.

The clock wound down to two minutes, one minute, 30 seconds. Trailing 22-19, Rags charged down the court toward the Falcons' basket on the far end of the court. He sent a long pass to John who tossed up a desperate, two-handed shot.

"There are 25 seconds left, John," Coach Buckwell called calmly to his son. "Get a better shot than that." Ben, still pacing the stairs, threw his head back in despair and pounded the tiled wall with his fist. The shot missed the rim, the backboard, everything, but landed squarely in the chest of a very surprised Austin. After staring at the ball for a second, he was spurred into action by a dozen cries from the parents' section far down the court.

Austin eyed the basket, hesitated, and then shuffled the ball to Pablo, who was standing just a foot away. Pablo, who had been getting in position for a possible rebound, nearly dropped the unexpected pass. But he managed to bank the ball off the backboard and into the net.

"All right, Pablo!" shouted Ben. After anxiously checking the scoreboard clock, he joined the screams of "Defense! Defense!"

Rags was scurrying from player to player like a waterbug, swiping and slapping at the ball. He tipped one pass but a Panther got to it first. More Falcons swarmed around the kid who picked up the ball.

"Don't foul him!" said Coach Buckwell.

The Panther twisted and turned but was surrounded by red jerseys, each of which seemed to have three hands. Instead of trying to pass the ball, he clutched it tight against his chest and bent over it with his body. After a few seconds, the referee signaled a jump ball.

"Who's going to jump it, ref?" shouted one parent. It was a good question. There were at least three Falcons who had tied up the Panthers.

"I hope it's not Rags," whispered Ben. As the shortest player on the floor, Rags could not hope to win a jump ball. The referee selected John for the jump-off. As the ball hung in the air, neither boy could gain control of the tap. The ball fell to the floor where Rags pounced on it.

"Time out!" called Coach Buckwell. There were nine seconds left. The Falcons huddled anxiously around their coach. "All right, all right. Here's what we're going to do," said the coach. There was no bickering or chatter as the players waited for the formula that would give them the win.

As the team waited, hardly daring to breath, the coach mulled over his options. The silence was hardest on Ben, who blurted out, "Put me in, Coach! I can make the shot. I don't have to drive into the middle or anything. All I have to do is stand out there and shoot it."

Coach's black eyebrows took on a menacing appearance as he turned to Ben. But then his look softened, as though Ben's suggestion had suddenly walked over and slugged him in the face.

Sensing the coach's hesitation for the first time, Ben stepped up the pressure. "I only have to stand and shoot, just like I've been doing in practice all week. There isn't a *chance* of getting hurt. I promise! Just pass me the ball and, boom! I shoot before anyone knows I have it."

As the referee blew the whistle summoning them back onto the court, Coach Buckwell finally spoke. "Okay, we'll try it. John, pass the ball in to Dave. Dave, get down the court fast and drop it off for Ben. Ben, you shoot and then back out of the way. The rest of you be ready for a rebound. You understand that, Ben? You're just shooting, nothing else!"

Ben nodded eagerly. He could hardly believe it! He was getting in the game, and with everything on the line. All he had to do was make his shot and the Falcons would win. He could show his face at school and not have to take any of Rudy's smart talk.

As Ben trotted off to center court, it never occurred to him that he might miss the shot. Number 14 in the black Panther uniform trotted toward him. "I'll have to lull this guy to sleep," Ben thought. Most of the parents were yelling encouragement to both sides as John tossed the ball in to Rags. The little guard zoomed down the court with a Panther right by his side.

Ben stood with his hands on his hips, as if he was just going to watch Rags take the ball to the hoop.

43

His defender turned to watch, too. Just then Ben took two quick steps toward the middle. The defender, caught by surprise, dashed after him. As he did, Ben stopped, took two steps the other way and held his arms out for the ball. The defender was still several steps away when Ben lofted his shot.

The ball ripped through the net cleanly with two seconds to spare. Ben ran and jumped across the court toward his coach as if powerful electrodes were wired to his shorts. Some of his teammates leaped off the stage and ran toward him with their fists pumping the air. But Coach Buckwell grabbed the leaders by the backs of their jerseys and jerked them back.

"His foot, his foot! Come on, don't go jumping on him! Hey, get off the court! There's still two seconds left."

Ben, grinning broadly, accepted hand slaps from all the Falcons on the bench. The team was so excited that no one remembered to take Ben's place on defense for the last two seconds. Fortunately, the Panthers were unable to get the ball across midcourt. The Falcons hopped up and down like a batch of red-coated popcorn bursting with the excitement of the win.

They savored the win for nearly ten minutes, exchanging their personal stories of what happened in those final seconds. The Falcons finally broke off and attached themselves to their parents. Ben was riding with Rags's parents tonight. When it seemed they were ready to go, he searched for his coat in a corner of the stage.

Stuffed in the pocket was a familiar blue envelope. Ben stepped back behind a stage curtain and ripped open the envelope. Reading hastily, before Rags or Pablo could see him, he found that same childish scrawl that he had seen before.

"Congratulations on waiting it out! Now you'll be free to play. May your season bring you all the joy you have hoped for. The Order of the Broken Arrow."

Following Pablo's hint that the letters were from a girl, Ben had meant to keep these notes a secret. But this one did not sound like anything a girl would write. It sounded more like an adult. He stuffed the letter in his pocket. As he came out from behind the curtain, he scanned the gym for clues as to who might be writing him notes. Nobody seemed to be giving any secret, sly glances or pretending that they did not notice him.

This is really weird, he thought.

5
A Suspect

It was a toss-up as to which was gloomier—the cold gymnasium lit up only by a row of small windows near the ceiling, or Austin Lund's face. This private practice session with Ben, two days before the end of winter break, was the worst yet.

It was not Austin's play that was so depressing. In fact, his free throw shooting had improved, he was catching the ball better, and he was starting to learn some things about playing defense. But Austin had arrived a few minutes late without a trace of spring in his step. It took him forever to peel off his coat. When Ben tossed him the basketball, Austin's expression reminded him of the way April looked at a pile of broccoli on her plate.

Every movement seemed to be an effort for Austin. But the worst part was that he didn't remember anything. He would nod while Ben spoke about using his body to shield the ball from defenders. But just 30 seconds later he would hold the ball right out where Ben could slap it away.

46

"Is something bugging you?" Ben asked. "You've been out to lunch ever since you showed up here."

Austin gulped and said, "Well, you see, I've been thinking about this quite a bit, and I don't really know if I'm into basketball all that much. I mean, let's face it, the whole thing has been pretty much of a disaster."

"I keep telling you that's just because you're new at it. Look how much better you're getting. You just have to keep working. It'll come."

"So will the glaciers, if you give them enough time," said Austin. "I just don't know if it's worth all the time I'm putting into it."

"You can't get anything really worthwhile in life without paying the price," Ben said. He felt a little odd giving someone else one of the very lines that he hated getting from his parents. Well, if that's what it took to keep from losing the tallest player in the league, that's what Ben would do.

"On the other hand," sighed Austin, "there's no sense in beating a dead horse. I don't exactly get the feeling that the one reason God put me on this earth was to play basketball."

"He made you tall, didn't He?" challenged Ben.

"I'm not sure that has anything to do with it," Austin said. For the first time since Ben had known him, Austin shook off his timid posture and started to get angry. "Look, God gave me a big nose, too. Does that mean I'm supposed to be a comedian? I get pretty tired of people telling me what I'm

47

supposed to do just because of how I look."

"No one's forcing you to do anything," Ben said, innocently. "I just thought you might like some extra help so you could make use of your size and really help the team. If you don't care about that, fine."

"I appreciate all the help you're giving me, Ben. But it's just too much. I can't be spending so much time at it. I've been so busy with this I haven't had any time to even do my art lessons, and my parents are paying a lot of money for those."

Art lessons? Ben almost laughed at the idea. *How could someone as awkward as Austin ever learn how to handle a paintbrush? He'd probably miss the paper half the time.* "You mean you're quitting the team?" he asked.

"I didn't say that," Austin replied. "I know I'm not much good, but it is kind of fun being on a team. You know, a bunch of guys all pulling for each other; it's really a different feeling. After you made that last shot to win the other night and we were all going wild, that was great! I don't mind the regular practices and I like getting a chance to play every game. It's just that—" Austin started fidgeting and his gaze dropped to the floor.

"You don't want any more of these extra practices," sighed Ben. So much for the big center they needed to win the championship.

"Yeah, I guess that's it," Austin said sheepishly. "You never seem to get tired of basketball but I just can't take so much of it."

48

"Fine," Ben shrugged, trying to hide his disappointment. "Just trying to help."

Austin straightened up as though a heavy weight had been lifted from his shoulders. "Want to finish with a free throw contest? Best out of 20 shots?"

Ben accepted the challenge and easily won, making 14 shots to Austin's 7. As they scooped up their jackets, Austin found a blue envelope lying next to their boots. "What's this? It's got your name on it."

Ben stared at the envelope. No one else had entered the gym the whole time they were practicing. "Did you see anyone come in here when you showed up?" Austin shook his head. "Somebody keeps slipping me secret notes. Whoever's doing it would make a great spy." He opened the note and read it.

"No matter where you go, no matter what you do, we are always thinking of you. The Order of the Secret Arrow." The whole goofy thing was starting to get on his nerves. He showed the note to Austin.

Austin's eyes grew wide with horror. "Sounds like a death threat! You think the Panthers are mad at you for that last shot?"

"No," laughed Ben. "I thought they were love notes at first. Maybe they still are, but they're so strange. I can't figure it out. I guess I'm just stuck with a secret admirer. Sure wish I knew who it was, though. Seems like a younger kid, especially with handwriting like that. But the words sound too grown up."

49

"Wow! It must really be something to be such a star," said Austin, shaking his head.

The notes kept coming. Ben had come to expect finding them at practice, but the matter really got serious when he opened his school locker and a blue envelope fluttered to the ground. Rags happened to be with him and he shook his head in bewilderment.

"They're everywhere," Rags chuckled. "Somebody really has it for you bad, Oak. It's almost scary."

Ben read the message, which was very similar to all the others. Then he ripped it into tiny pieces and dropped them in a wastebasket.

"This has gone a little bit too far," Ben said. "I don't mind having a fan club, but I don't like the idea of somebody on my tail everywhere I go."

"So what are you going to do?" Rags asked.

"I need some help," Ben said. "Whoever it is always waits until I'm not looking before making a move. They're sneaky enough so that I can't catch them. What I need is for you and Pablo to keep an eye out for me. You might be able to spot them doing something while my back is turned."

"I can't spend the whole day out in the hall watching your locker," Rags said.

"Neither can the note sender," said Ben. "I just want you to keep an eye on my locker whenever you happen to be out in the hall. Let me know if you see anything strange going on."

"If I told you everything strange I saw going on in this school, we'd never have time for anything else."

"Just do it, would you?"

Rags saluted. "Yessir. I won't let you down, sir."

"And tell Pablo."

It was Pablo who came bursting into the lunchroom with the report two days later. "Oak! Rub my head, would you? Maybe some of what you got will rub off on me!"

Ben let the bite of peanut butter sandwich rest in his mouth for a moment. "What is your problem?"

"My problem is that Ms. Marinetti isn't in love with me."

Just then Rags trotted through the doors, scanned the room for a moment, and rushed over to them. A stern glance from the principal slowed him to a fast walk, but he was nearly breathless when he reached Ben. Rubbing his friend's shoulders like a trainer soothing a prizefighter he said, "Oak, you sly fox! How do you do it?!"

Staring up at his two grinning friends, Ben swallowed the sandwich and said, "Is your disease contagious?"

"I sure hope yours is," said Pablo, grabbing his hand. "Here, touch me!"

"I'm sorry to hear about the loss of your brain," said Ben, turning away from them. "But then I heard you weren't really very close to it anyway. Let me know when you get back to reality."

51

Pablo and Rags pulled out chairs, one on each side of Ben. "We did it, Oak," said Pablo. "Superspies at your service. We found out who your secret lover is."

"She really messed up this time," added Rags. "Pablo and I were at opposite ends of the hall and we both saw her slip a *blue envelope* under the door of your locker. Caught her red-handed, both of us."

"Really?" Ben didn't know which of his friends to turn to. "So come on, already. Who is it?"

"You sly dog," said Rags.

"We should make him pay," said Pablo to Rags. "This info's worth a fortune. We'd never have to work for the rest of our lives."

"If you don't tell me now, there won't be any rest of your lives to worry about."

Rags and Pablo grinned at each other. "Are you ready?" asked Pablo. "It's Ms. Marinetti!"

"Very funny," said Ben, sarcastically. It was ridiculous enough that they chose someone from the school staff as the supposed letter writer. But Ms. Marinetti, the new librarian, was the most gorgeous woman any of them had ever seen. "Big joke."

"We're not playing with you, man!" said Rags.

"Get this!" said Pablo, sitting on the end of his seat. "I'm coming up the stairs and the first thing I see is Ms. Marinetti kneeling on the floor shoving a blue envelope in the bottom of your locker."

"I swear it's the truth!" said Rags. "I saw it, too."

"You guys, this isn't even funny," sneered Ben.

"Okay, you don't believe us?" said Pablo. "You know that powerful perfume she's always wearing? Run by the library and get a whiff of it and see if it ain't the same stuff that rubbed off on the letter."

Ben still didn't really believe it, but if these two were acting, they were doing a better job than usual. When he got to his locker, there was a corner of a blue envelope hanging out. Ben pulled it out and read, "These notes are just to let you know how special you are. Enjoy the day. Order of the Broken Arrow." Ben ran the envelope by his nose and, sure enough, there was an unmistakable scent to it.

"You sly fox," Rags said, chucking him under the chin.

6

Miscalculation

Ben finished the school day in a daze. Ms. Marinetti in love with him? There were movie stars who would have given anything to have her looks. He knew he was in way over his head on this one. "Come on, I'm just a kid," he kept saying to himself. The whole notion had him so dumbfounded that he was glad he had a basketball game that night. If there was one thing that could get his mind off Ms. Marinetti for a while, it was basketball.

Unfortunately, while Ben was running through a pregame lay-up drill, he spotted her coming through the double doors of the gym. Rags saw it, too, and as he flipped a rebound to Ben he said, "Sly dog!"

Ben could not believe it. Here was the moment he had been waiting for. After all these months of waiting and six weeks of nursing an injured foot, he was finally going to do what he loved best in life—play a game of basketball. And now something had come up that totally distracted him. *She* was here to watch him play.

His walk took on a slightly cocky swagger as he tried to live up to the role that had been thrust on him. He decided that he would put on a show for her that she would never forget.

The Richland Raiders were a well-coached team. Unlike many players who would pass only when it was certain they could not get a shot off, the Raiders passed the ball around, looking for a good shot. Even with Ben joining Rags at the guard position, the Falcons' full court press was unable to force many turnovers. If not for the fact that the Raiders missed a large number of open shots, the Falcons would have been in deep trouble.

As it was, Ben was able to match points with them. Drawing extra strength as he felt the eyes of Ms. Marinetti on him, he kept driving into the lane for lay-ups, or faking a drive and firing up a longer shot. By the end of the first quarter, he had already scored 12 points, more than the Falcons' entire team had scored in their first game.

Sitting on the bench in the second quarter, Ben risked several sidelong glances towards Ms. Marinetti. She was playing it as cagey as ever. In fact, she was going out of her way to make it look as though she were really cheering for the Raiders. When they tied the score just before halftime, she even jumped to her feet and clapped her hands.

Nice act, he smiled to himself. *But you're wasting your breath. I'm wise to you now.*

Having served his time on the bench, Ben

expected to play the entire second half. This time they would be going for the basket right in front of Ms. Marinetti. *Yessir, Ms. Marinetti,* he thought. *Sit back and enjoy the show. There's no way these clowns are going to stay with us.*

The Falcons wasted no time in regaining the lead. Rags forced a bad pass in the Raiders' backcourt. Ben intercepted and laid it in for the score. It was all he could do to resist looking to see her reaction.

Ben felt so strong and sure of himself that he almost toyed with the defenders. Even when he was double-teamed, he could sometimes get both opponents off balance with a clever fake. He missed a couple of shots, though, and after a third straight miss, he was angry enough at himself that he bulled over a couple of Raiders to get the rebound.

The referee blew his whistle and called out "Red, number 22, over the back on the rebound. Blue team's ball." Ben stared at the referee for a moment with a sarcastic smile. Then he shook his head as he retreated downcourt for defense.

Coach Buckwell finally took him out of the game with two minutes to go. But as he slumped into the chair feeling pleasantly fatigued, he knew the game was over. The Falcons were ahead 37 to 30. He glanced back up at Ms. Marinetti and saw her smiling and talking to a woman sitting next to her. He knew he must have made her proud. By his own unofficial count, he had scored 28 points, nearly enough to beat the Raiders all by himself.

"This is the life," he thought. "Man, I love basketball!" Having someone like Ms. Marinetti backing him was frosting on an already delicious cake. "It's nice someone cares about what I do," Ben thought. His own parents had not even bothered to show up.

The game ended at 38 to 34. Ben hardly noticed the congratulations from his teammates, and his mind was too busy with other things to offer many himself. He was more curious to see what Ms. Marinetti had put in the note that he knew he would find in his boots.

"Pretty soon maybe we'll be able to talk. Hope you enjoyed your game. Thinking of you, Order of the Broken Arrow."

"Wow!" said Ben.

"If I were you, I'd ask her to marry me quick, before she changes her mind about you," said Pablo.

"Would you stop being such a dork?" said Ben. But he could not help feeling proud. Of all the guys in the whole school, or in the whole world, who thought Ms. Marinetti was a knockout, it was he, Ben Oakland, who had the rights to her.

The three of them were squeezing their way through the front hall traffic toward the waiting buses. "The note said she wanted to talk to you, man," Rags said. "So what are you waiting for? She's probably all alone in the library."

"Chicken!" said Pablo.

Somehow having Ms. Marinetti in the palm of his

hand brought out the daring in Ben. Without a word of explanation, he left his two grinning friends standing in the bus line and threaded his way through the crowd toward the stairway.

Ms. Marinetti was not exactly alone in the library. But the five or six students sharing the wide open spaces of the room with her were spread out far enough away that it would be possible to hold a private conversation. She was sitting underneath a buzzing fluorescent ceiling panel, logging in some data on a computer terminal. Her blonde hair was curled back from the sides of her face and her long eyelashes blinked frequently as she studied the data.

Ben walked toward her. His heart suddenly jumped as he picked up the scent of that perfume. She gave no hint of noticing him. He felt foolish just standing there, so he picked up a reference book that happened to be nearby.

Several times he glanced up at her, and finally she happened to look up as well. Ben's mouth instantly dried into a desert. "Hi," he croaked.

"Hi, Ben," she smiled. "Anything I can help you with?"

Ben reminded himself that she was the one who was crazy about him. "Maybe," he said innocently. "Is there anything I can help you with?"

She raised a curious eyebrow as she typed in some more numbers. "Ach, dummy!" she said, erasing some numbers off the screen. "Well, are you any good at databases?"

"I don't know, I'm pretty good with computers," he said, coming around the side of the desk.

Ms. Marinetti stared at him as he crossed into her forbidden work space. Then she laughed and jabbed at a few more keys. "That's all right. I'd better do it myself. That's what they pay me for. Are you sure there isn't something you need?"

"Well, we could talk," he said smugly, taking his cue.

Ms. Marinetti swept a lock of hair back and stared blankly into space. "I get a lot of requests during a day, but this is a new one on me."

"It seems to me it was someone else's idea."

The librarian looked past his shoulder to see if someone were lurking around the doorway. Seeing no one, she sat in silence for a few seconds and then said, "Do you really have something to do in here or are you just playing games?"

Enough of this playing around, thought Ben. "Well, I just wanted to let you know that I really appreciated the notes," he said.

"I'm flattered," she said, studying the sheaf of papers again. "I hope that means you'll return those books before the end of the year."

Ben cleared his throat. "I have two witnesses who saw you put a blue envelope in my locker."

Ms. Marinetti broke into such a high-pitched laugh that the kids in the far end of the library turned to look at them. "So, that's what you're talking about. Don't mention it. Glad to do it."

59

"It is confusing, though," said Ben, coyly, closing in on the subject. "I mean, why was it written in children's handwriting?"

"I give up," said the librarian, as if she were the model of patience. "Why was it written in children's handwriting?"

"Are you going to pretend you don't remember what the note said?"

Ms. Marinetti's tolerant smile vanished. As she stared squarely into Ben's eyes, he suddenly felt as shaky as if the library rug had turned to quicksand. "I don't care for what you're implying. I don't read other people's notes. I saw the note sticking way out of your locker. Someone brushed against it, knocked it out, and I picked it up and put it back."

"Just kidding," Ben said, with a hollow laugh. He felt the shame rising into his face and it felt hot as molten lava. Now he was confused, unsure. But what about the basketball game last night? Trying to wiggle out of the idiotic spot he had blundered into, he cleared his throat and said, "Actually, I just came to say I saw you at the basketball game last night."

Ms. Marinetti's anger had gone but the smile that reappeared on her face had left behind a good deal of its warmth. "That's right, you were playing for that red team, weren't you?"

"I, uh, just wanted to ask what you were doing there."

Leaning on one elbow the librarian said, wearily, "My boyfriend coaches the Raiders. Now is there anything else about my personal life that I haven't covered?"

Ben felt like his head was so full of blood that it sloshed when he shook it. He shrugged and said, "Bye" and walked out of the room, lashed by pangs of shame. If the earth was not kind enough to swallow him up, he planned to take the next flight out of the country to some remote place where no one knew what kind of a total idiot he was. By the time he walked all the way home in the cold shadows of a waning sun, he had calmed down a little. But he was certain he would never enter another library for as long as he lived.

7

Good Shots

"Coach Peters, there's a spy in here!" Rudy Trabor announced over the echoing thunder of a dozen bouncing basketballs.

"What are you talking about?" asked the physical education teacher. Mr. Peters was a walking advertisement for either shampoo or hair spray. His styled black hair always looked freshly clipped and it seemed locked into combed position.

Rudy pointed toward a figure in the doorway. "That's one of the players on the team we're going to beat tomorrow," he said, loudly enough that Ben could hear him.

Mr. Peters looked at Ben and smiled. "Doesn't bother me. We don't have any gimmicks or secret plays." Turning to his team, he said, "It's all you fellows can do to just learn the basics. And if we don't have a better practice today than we did last time, Ben should find it very entertaining. Maybe it's a good thing he's here. After watching you clowns, he'll go back and tell his team about what a

62

bunch of bozos the Pine Knoll Knicks are, and they'll get so overconfident that maybe we'll have a chance."

Ben smiled to himself. Mr. Peters was his idea of a coach. The man knew what he was talking about, took no nonsense from anyone, and his practice sessions were all business. Compared to him, Mr. Buckwell was just a motorist studying his road map, trying to figure out how to get back to the main road.

Contrary to what Mr. Peters had suggested, Ben saw nothing in the practice session that made him overconfident. Greg Murphy was a deadly shot and he got rid of the ball so quickly that it would be tough to stop him. "I'm guarding him," Ben thought, his nerves starting to jump as he considered the challenge. Rudy and Rich Silas both had talent to go with their height. Rudy was especially strong and he played hard. Ben could see that Pablo and Austin were going to get worked over.

The Falcons' only chance was to stop the Knick guards before they could feed their big men under the basket. At least Coach Buckwell had been aware of his team's shortcomings and insisted that they practice that full court press. If a team could outshoot and outrebound you, your only hope was to try to force them to make mistakes. "Rags and I will pick them clean," Ben vowed, grimly.

He knew he should have left before the practice ended. But he could not resist hearing Mr. Peters's little pep talk at the end. Coach Buckwell never gave pep talks. "Just remember, the people who start the game aren't necessarily the ones who will finish it," Mr. Peters was saying, his chin jutting out, daring anyone to challenge him. "I'll be watching to see who really wants to play ball. The people who want to work hard and do what they're supposed to are the ones who play on my team. Remember, eat a light meal at about five and be at this gym by 6 p.m. If you come later than that, don't expect to play."

Ben zipped up his jacket and began to walk out the double doors thinking about what might have been if he had joined the Knicks. It was hard to believe that both the Falcons and the Knicks were 4-1. Ben felt like a volunteer fire fighter who had just watched the professionals in action.

"Hey, Oakland!" called Rudy, before Ben could escape. Ben pretended to ignore him and kept walking slowly down the hall. Once upon a time he had gotten along reasonably well with Rudy, but lately the kid had been pretty obnoxious. Pablo said it was because Rudy had expected Ben to join the Pine Knoll team and had bragged that they were going to go undefeated.

Rudy followed him into the hall just far enough to yell, "We're going to wipe the court with you guys!"

Ben turned and smiled. "Your coach doesn't seem to think so. See you around, Bozo."

"He's just bluffing," said Rudy with half a sneer

curled across his freckled lips. "Too bad you joined the losers when you could have been on a winner."

Ben laughed. "Our record's the same as yours. Better put some pants on. It's cold out here in the hall. Wouldn't want you to get sick and miss the big game."

Rudy's deep brown eyes overflowed with spite. "I hear you tried to make a basketball player out of that big ox. Didn't work, did it?"

This guy's really a moron, thought Ben, angrily. "I'd rather have Austin on my team than you any day," he snapped.

"You won't be saying that after I get through with him tomorrow," leered Rudy.

"He can outplay you any day," Ben shot back. Immediately, he knew it was a stupid thing to say. Austin couldn't outplay a fence post half the time, much less Rudy. But Ben was not going to stand there and listen to someone make fun of his teammates.

"Ho, ho!" scoffed Rudy, twirling his sweatshirt around his index finger. "Care to put some money on that? Twenty dollars says I outscore and outrebound him at least three to one. Make it four to one."

Ben's eyes narrowed in hatred. Mr. Hotshot had him boxed in now. Ben would never live it down if he backed off his support of Austin. On the other hand, betting on Austin was like betting on an ice cube to freeze a blast furnace.

The lean, muscular form of Mr. Peters appeared around the corner to save the day. "You want to bet on games, you'll do it from the sidelines," he said to Rudy. "I don't need ball players who mouth off. If there's any talking to be done, the coach does it. Understand?"

Ben wished he could see Rudy's face, but the boy was facing the coach and pulling a sweatshirt over his head. *Serves him right,* he thought, biting his cheeks to keep from laughing out loud. *We'll see who picked a bunch of losers!*

That night Ben went out after supper and shot baskets in the shadowy light of an outdoor lamppost. For more than an hour he pumped shot after shot at the hoop. *I'll beat those Knicks by myself if I have to,* he thought.

Only the sight of Ken's desk lit up in their bedroom window saved him from disaster. Tossing the ball back into the garage, he raced upstairs and finished his math assignment at two minutes before nine. There was no doubt in his mind that his parents would have banned him from the big game if he had been so much as a minute late.

It felt funny being the visiting team on his own school court. It made the place look different. Ben was not sure if it was because he had never been in there at night, or whether it came from being surrounded by teammates he had only seen in a church setting. The floor seemed shinier and the gymnasium smaller than usual. It even seemed as though he had to make adjustments in his shot to keep the ball from bouncing too hard off the backboard. Strange, he had never had any trouble with that backboard before.

While retrieving a ball that had been struck in midflight by another ball, Ben watched Austin warm up. For a moment he studied him with Rudy's critical eye. No grace or quickness. Rudy would eat him up. If only Austin could somehow block a shot, then Rudy might be intimidated by those long arms hovering above him. It was not impossible. Austin was so tall that he had managed to block a couple in the Falcons' last game without leaving his feet. Actually, that was the only way he could block a shot, because he never did leave his feet.

Austin took a couple of dribbles and then swung his arm in an arc over his head. The ball swished through the net. He broke into a wide smile, which he shared with Ben. "Finally nailed one of those buggers," he said.

"You ready to try one in a game?" he asked hopefully.

Austin's brow furrowed in a deep, soul-searching meditation. His smile resurfaced a few seconds later accompanied by a weak nod. Ben did not take that as a promising sign. *Sure, he'll take the shot, but he doesn't expect to make it*, he thought. *That isn't going to help us much tonight.*

67

After shooting just enough to get loose, Ben returned to the folding chairs that had been set up for the Falcons. He did not want to waste any of his strength. As he sat there, loosening his laces to straighten out the tongue of his shoe, Coach Buckwell crossed the floor and sat next to him.

For a few moments the coach stared silently as if his thoughts had been left behind on the other side of the court. Then he focused on Ben and said, "You know, you took quite a few shots last game."

"Made quite a few, too," Ben said, defensively.

"Yeah, well, they weren't all good shots. And the rest of the team was standing around waiting for you to score." Ben had never really talked to Coach Buckwell at this close range before. Now he could see the jowls shaking as Coach chewed his gum. "It gets them into bad habits. Did you see how lost they looked on offense whenever you left the game?"

"I don't have to leave the game," Ben said. "I never get tired."

The coach raised one of his droopy eyelids higher than Ben had seen them before. "This team isn't called 'Ben Oakland and His Faith Falcons,' " he went on, in his patient, halting voice. "We've got to find playing time for everyone, and we've got to find shots for other players."

"I don't think the others mind," Ben said, trying to copy the coach's patience. "After all, they want to win."

Coach started to speak, then cleared his throat.

"Yes, they want to win. And I think our chances are better if you don't play one against five on offense."

Ben, who had expected to win this argument easily, grew irritated at the coach's insistence that he change his style of play. Well, it was a poor time to ask for this. He had already calculated that he would have to play the game of his life and score at least 30 points in order for the Falcons to beat the Pine Knoll Knicks. If he started giving up shots to other players, it was as good as handing the ball over to the Knicks.

Ben's silence had given Coach a chance to collect some more thoughts. "Instead of trying to shoot with two guys hanging all over you, take advantage of it," the coach said as blandly as if he were asking Ben to pass him a container of water. "If there are two guys on you, that means one of your teammates is wide open. Do what you've been doing and get the defense to come after you. Then dump to the open man."

"Sure," said Ben, looking away. "I'm not a ball hog. I don't care who gets the points, just so we get them. As long as our guys can make their shots, I'll feed them all night long. But if they don't, then it's up to me." *There, that ought to settle him*, he thought. *What could be more reasonable?*

"The goal is to get good shots," insisted Coach. "The team that gets the most good shots usually wins. If we miss the good shots, we miss. There's nothing you can do about it. But that doesn't mean we ever stop playing for the good shots."

What's the point of arguing? thought Ben. He nodded to the coach and trotted back onto the court to warm up. *I'll try it for a while*, he thought, watching Rudy jump for a rebound and then snap a pass to another Knick. *But this is one game we have to win.*

Coach Buckwell collected the team around him a few minutes later. As usual, he asked for quiet several times before he found something to say. "Okay, boys. Starters will be Dave and Ben at the guards, Chris and John at forward, Paul at center. Remember to play full court press all the time; we'll need it. Don't worry about getting tired, we'll get a fresh player in for you."

Like the rest of the team, Ben was waiting for something more. But the coach had apparently said all that he planned to. He sat back in his chair and scribbled some notes down on his pad.

"Play ball!" said the referee, after a sharp blast on his whistle. The referee was a big guy with a crew cut and a forehead that looked like it was carved out of rock. *No one's going to pull anything past this drill sergeant*, Ben thought as he trotted out to the jump circle. Immediately he sought out Greg Murphy.

"Hi, Ben. Are you guarding me?" Greg asked, tucking in his blue shirt and smoothing some of the crinkles out of his gold shorts.

"Only when I don't have the ball," said Ben.

"Want to give up now so I don't have to wear myself out?"

"Nah, go ahead. Wear yourself out."

"How come Rudy's so quiet?" Ben whispered to Greg. Rudy was waiting inside the center circle, hands on his hips. When Pablo arrived for the jump, Rudy simply shook his hand and then crouched into position.

"He won't be if we win," Greg whispered back.

Pablo jumped high for the opening tip, but Rudy was four inches taller and won it easily. No sooner did Casey Pendleton grab the ball for the Knicks, however, than Rags was all over him.

"A little help! A little help!" Coach Peters was yelling to his Knicks. Greg immediately ran back toward his teammate. Ben jogged behind him, giving Greg plenty of room, inviting the pass. Before the ball even left Casey's hands, Ben made his move. He cut in front of Greg, tapped the ball with his fingers and sprinted after it. Catching up to it just before it rolled out of bounds, he stopped and layed it in for two points.

Was that a good enough shot, Coach? Or should I have passed it? he chuckled to himself as he looked back down the court toward both benches.

"Press!" shouted Rags, jumping in to harass the Knicks as they tried to pass the ball in bounds.

Almost forgot, Ben thought, turning around to find Greg. This time the Knicks were able to break through, although John nearly deflected a pass into

71

Chris's hands. The Knick guards were already so flustered by the Falcons' attacking defense that they were not even thinking about getting a shot. It was all they could do to keep the Falcons from getting the ball. One of the Knicks finally kicked the ball away before they were even able to take a shot.

"Time out!" shouted Coach Peters. Ben was so fascinated by the tongue-lashing that the Knicks were getting during the time-out that he didn't even hear what his own coach was saying. It didn't matter much; Coach Buckwell didn't really have anything to say except "Good work" and "Keep it up." Coach Peters, meanwhile, was loudly demanding to know who wanted to play tonight and who didn't care, adding his opinion that there were many more in the second category than the first. The coach seemed so genuinely upset that Ben began to wonder if it really was so much fun playing for him after all.

After the time-out, the Falcons brought the ball downcourt. The Knicks tried to answer the Falcons' full court press with one of their own. That lasted only as long as it took Rags to speed past two defenders and race downcourt. Leaving blue-shirted bodies lying in his wake, Rags steamed toward the basket and flipped the ball to an unguarded Pablo. Pablo easily sank the shot. Ben rightly guessed that it was the last time the Falcons would see the press that game.

Pine Knoll finally worked the ball in close to the

hoop to Rich Silas. His shot from close range bounced off the rim, but Rudy grabbed the rebound. His quick flip from the left-hand side of the basket also bounced out, but he again came away with the rebound. His second follow-up shot rolled around the rim and in. The Knicks were on the scoreboard.

Under newly shouted orders from their coach, the Knicks hurried back to guard their basket and let Rags walk the ball upcourt. As Ben had expected, Greg guarded him closely. No problem; he could get rid of Greg. But no sooner had he caught the ball and dribbled around Greg than Rudy stepped in to block his path.

Rather than trying to shoot over his tall opponent, Ben dribbled away from the basket. Again he drove around Greg only to run straight into Rudy, who had stepped out to meet him. *That means that someone's open*, he thought. It wasn't Pablo, who was working under the shadow of the much taller Rich. That meant Chris was unguarded.

After faking a pass to Rags, Ben zipped a pass to Chris. Ben's fake had fooled more than just the defense, though. Chris was staring straight at Rags when the ball hit him in the chest and bounced out-of-bounds. "How about that?" Ben muttered, resuming his argument with the coach. "Was that what you call a good shot?"

The Knicks missed an outside shot, but again four long arms branched out over Pablo's outstretched hands. Two of them belonged to Rich, who wrestled the ball away from his teammate Rudy and banked an easy shot off the backboard to tie the game at 4-4. "They're doin' a lot of shoving under the basket," Ben complained to the referee, who ignored him.

Again, Ben charged into the lane. This time he knew what to expect. *Here comes those freckly legs*, he thought as Rudy moved toward him. Ben shoved a pass to the unguarded Chris near the sideline. Although he stood less than eight feet from the basket, Chris hesitated and looked for Ben.

"Shoot it!" screamed Ben.

As if the ball had suddenly grown hot, Chris instantly flung the ball well over the basket. Not only did the miss give the ball back to the Knicks, it seemed to ungag Rudy's mouth. "Air ball!" he said, mockingly as he collected the miss and handed it to Casey.

Before he could complete the handoff, Rags zipped in from nowhere. He slapped the ball away and went up for the shot. He missed, but the embarrassed Rudy fouled him, and Rags was awarded two shots.

While Rudy was being yanked from the game by an irate coach, Rags Yamagita made one of his two foul shots to put the Falcons back on top. It remained a close contest throughout much of the first half, until Rags, and then Ben were taken out. The Falcon substitutes were not as effective with their press, and the Knicks were able to move the ball inside to take advantage of their height.

After Rudy and Rich played volleyball rebounding each other's misses, Coach Buckwell turned to Austin. "They're killing us under the basket. We need some height."

Never before had Rags, Pablo, and Ben all been on the bench at the same time. Never before had Chris, Nathan, John, Donny, and Austin all been out on the court at one time. The three friends stared at each other glumly as the Knicks moved out to a 16-11 lead. "We don't have anyone in there who can score," muttered Pablo.

"At least they're getting good shots," Ben snorted sarcastically.

By the time Rags returned to the game, the Knicks' lead had grown to 20-11. Austin had not played badly on defense. In fact, he had pulled in one rebound and had stunned Rudy by blocking one of his shots. It was funny watching Austin lope down the court after making the block. "He's so excited you can almost detect some spring in his step," said Rags.

Ben did not return to action in the first half. While he watched, grinding his teeth at the sorry spectacle, the Pine Knoll Knicks pulled away to a 23-11 lead at halftime. The worst part of it was that Rudy was starting to play with that sick, cocky "I told you so" grin of his.

8
The Lay-up

That did it! The Knicks were going to die! So much for these good shots that his teammates were so scared to take! Those guys had not scored any more points with Ben passing off than they had in the last game when he had been shooting the ball. Meanwhile, Ben had totaled only four points. The Knicks were sure to be having a good laugh about that. *A good shot is a shot that has a chance of going in*, he decided. *It doesn't matter where Chris or Rags shoot from. They can't make it so it's automatically a bad shot. Anything I shoot has a good chance of going in. Therefore any shot I take is a good shot.*

Ben began firing from the opening moments of the second half. More than that, he had decided to take charge on defense. When the Knicks were on offense, he would guard Greg only until the ball went into the middle. Then he would charge in and try to strip the ball away from the Knicks' two tall players. The tactic worked well. Along with several steals they gained off their press, the Falcons were able to slice the lead to 26-24 by the end of the third quarter.

To his surprise, Ben found himself on the sidelines for the start of the last period. As he sat there, burning the coach with an accusing stare, Coach Buckwell said, "You're playing hard. You need a rest. For crying out loud, you don't have to do everything yourself."

"Wanna' bet?" Ben felt like saying.

One person who was playing more than usual was Austin. Although he still appeared to be thinking out each move, the big guy was actually posing some problems for Rich and Rudy. They were so used to being the tallest players on the court that neither knew much about how to get a shot off against a taller player.

Austin looked so much more comfortable on the court than he ever had before that Ben almost risked a pass to him. The big fingers were outstretched, almost as if he *wanted* the ball, and he was shielding his opponent with his body. Ben started throwing the ball to him, then thought better of it. The memory of too many bumbled passes in practice was still too fresh. Instead he dribbled left, dribbled right, dribbled left, and finally worked his way between three Knicks defenders. He flung up an off-balance shot that bounced high off the rim and went in. That closed the margin to 33-30.

Neither team was able to score for the next few

minutes. Finally, with two minutes to go, the full court press again claimed a victim. Lurching as if he were ready to drop from exhaustion, Rags hounded Casey into using up his dribble. As the Knicks' guard sought out someone to throw to, Rags punched the ball out of his hand. Both players dived for the ball. His face twisted with strain, Rags batted the ball away from Casey toward the free throw line.

Chris got there first and picked it up. He started to dribble, then saw Ben coming up behind him. As if caught red-handed stealing something that belonged to Ben, Chris shoved the ball at Ben, who made the lay-up.

Coach Buckwell immediately called time-out. He escorted the dazed Rags to a seat and sent in Nathan to take his place. "One point! One point!" said Ben as he rushed up to each of his teammates to encourage them. "Two minutes left, we're only down by one. Let's win this just the way we beat the Panthers."

First they had to stop the Knicks, and they had to do it without Rags. The little guy gamely offered to go back in but Coach Buckwell congratulated him on playing hard and sat him in the seat next to him. That was the seat reserved for someone who was not going to be playing.

For the next minute and a half, Ben played his own version of defense. Instead of playing man-to-man defense, it was more like man-to-ball defense. Ben simply went after whoever had the ball. He nearly stole the ball from Casey, and nearly forced a jump ball against Rich. But in the end, all he succeeded in doing was getting in the way of his teammates and tiring himself out.

Casey fired a quick pass to Rudy, who tossed it back to Greg near the free throw line. Because Ben had chased the pass toward Rudy, he was too far behind to recover. Greg was wide open for the shot. The Knicks' ace shooter, who had been shut down by Ben most of the night, dribbled one step closer and fired. With a tremendous effort, Austin ran in from the side and launched himself several inches off the floor. His long arm rose high in the air and struck the ball with a THWACK!

He blocked the shot so completely that the ball nearly stuck to his hand like flypaper. No one looked more surprised than Austin to see the ball wind up in his hands. As the Knicks retreated on defense, Austin held the ball proudly. It obviously had not occurred to him what to do next.

Ben shot an anxious glance at the scoreboard clock. Some of the numbers were not working on it, and it took two seconds before he figured out there were 19 seconds left. "Throw it here quick!" he shouted.

Austin did as he was told and Ben dribbled toward the waiting Knicks. His own teammates might as well have been invisible. Ben was looking only at blue and gold uniforms, trying to figure out how to get a shot off. After a couple of seconds, he decided to win the game just like he had before—a long shot would be better than trying to beat three or four Knicks up the middle. He charged forward, getting the Knicks defenders back on their heels. Suddenly he stopped and raised the ball just above his forehead.

It felt bad as soon as he let it go. Desperately he charged in for the rebound. But he stepped on Austin's foot and both of them fell heavily. Rudy was holding the ball high over his head as if it were a trophy fish.

Scrambling to his feet, Ben lunged at the ball. Just in time Rudy fired it downcourt to Rich. Ben could hear the seconds ticking down in his head. He raced downcourt to where Pablo was badgering Rich, arms waving like a willow in a storm. Rich tried to pass it to Greg but he floated a soft pass that John was able to intercept.

Ben saw the clock flash six seconds. "Throw it here quick!"

John did, but two Knicks stepped in to block Ben's path. There was no way he could get close enough for a good shot. He would be lucky to reach mid-court before the final whistle blew.

Suddenly he saw Austin limping near the free throw line far down the court. The collision with Ben had stunned him and he had been slow in getting up. In the mad scramble of the final seconds he had been left behind near the basket. Ben quickly fired a one-handed pass down the court.

It was coming hard and Austin put his hands in front of his ducking head to protect himself in case he missed. He did not catch it cleanly, but knocked it down and picked it upon the bounce. Three seconds left. All he needed to do was dribble in about five steps and lay the ball in to win.

Austin brought the ball up to his chest and crouched. Too late, Ben saw what was happening. "No!" he screamed in horror. Instead of driving in for the easy lay-up, Austin launched a shot from the spot at which he had caught the ball. The shot clanged high off the backboard and bounced to the left side. Austin chugged after it but by the time he retrieved it, the game was over.

Ben swung a fist wildly in the air and stamped a foot. Frustrated as he was, he would not say anything to Austin, of course. But how dumb could you get? *A simple lay-up,* he thought to himself. *That's all you had to do. We had this game won! Shoot, if you knew how to jump you could have dunked the ball!*

Not even a pat on the shoulder from the Knicks' coach could calm the rage that was boiling in his guts. "Nice game, Ben," said Mr. Peters. "Your guys played a great game. I don't think we deserved to beat you."

The gym teacher went on to congratulate the rest of the Falcons for their effort. Ben watched him with resentment. *Yeah, it's easy to be nice when you win. Unless, of course, your name is Rudy Trabor,*

81

he thought, catching sight of the freckly face. Rudy was strutting off the court with that sick grin. He aimed a finger at Ben as if it were a gun, pulled the trigger, then blew the smoke away from the barrel.

Sure, you weasel, Ben thought, turning away from him. *Lucky stiff!* Rudy was playing it smart. If he had dared come close to Ben with that stupid grin of his, Ben would have slugged him—he wouldn't have cared how many people saw him do it.

"Tough loss," said Ben's dad, offering him his sweat jacket. "You guys have nothing to be ashamed of."

Austin does, thought Ben. *Why couldn't it have been anyone else? Even Donny had at least a 50-50 chance of making a lay-up.* April and Nick were chasing each other around Dad's legs, yelping and giggling. Ben wished they'd have stayed home. All he needed now was some noisy kids getting on his nerves.

"Did you win?" asked April, sucking on some strands of her long hair.

"Yeah, we beat them 100 to nothing."

April's eyes grew wild and she immediately repeated the news to Nick before the two enjoyed a sprint across the wide-open spaces of the gym.

"Man, you sure put a scare into those guys," Ken said, walking over with Mom. Ben had not even seen Ken during the game; he wondered if he had come in late. "They thought it was going to be easy. Guess you showed them."

82

"They won, didn't they?" muttered Ben.

"Only as far as the final score," smiled Mom. "Why don't we celebrate with a trip to the Dairy Queen?"

"Celebrate what?" Ben grumped to himself. "Can't anyone around here read a scoreboard? We lost! I'll be hearing about it at school for the rest of the season." Memories of the game and especially those final 20 seconds so filled his brain that he failed to notice anything unusual as he slipped on his jacket. For once there was no secret message waiting for him at the end of a game.

9

Technical Foul

The radio station had given up trying to keep pace with the flood of cancellations being phoned in. "I think it's safe to assume that all events scheduled for today anywhere in the city and outlying areas have been cancelled," chuckled the announcer. The blizzard had dumped such an avalanche of snow on the city that only the extremely foolish, and those with four-wheel drive vehicles and a good reason for being out, tried to plow through the snow-clogged streets.

Many hearty souls who tried to get an early jump on their shoveling were quickly beaten back to the shelter of their homes by the bitter cold and the driving blasts of wind. Over the roar of the arctic fury, Ben could only occasionally make out the drone of a faraway snowblower.

Throughout the entire block there were only two ribbons of concrete that had been shoveled out from under the snow. One was a portion of driveway near the end of the block. It had been cleared by an overeager man who had promptly gotten his car stuck in the street after traveling all of four yards. Some helpful neighbors pushed the car back to the garage, and the driveway was fast filling up with a fresh dump of snow.

The other cleared area was the basketball court on the driveway at 2134 West Sheridan Avenue, dug out moments ago by Ben Oakland. Ben was sweating heavily even as he tucked his chin further into his collar to keep it from freezing. Wearing a stocking cap underneath his hood, with only his eyes and part of his nose poking out from under a scarf, Ben leaned the shovel against the side of the house and began shooting at the basket.

After a gust of wind carried one of his shots nearly to the roof, Ben confined his practice to short- and medium-range attempts. He kept wiggling his fingers in his gloves in an effort to ward off frostbite. Occasionally he had to pull his fingers out of their slots and clench them together to bring some warmth back to them.

The ball hardly bounced and it felt as hard as a brick when he rebounded a missed shot. But he was too busy replaying the last loss to take much notice of either the weather or the frozen ball. His mind had set up a two-man obstacle course between himself and the basket. There was Greg; there was Rudy.

For nearly half an hour, he spun and twirled, trying to keep control of the low-bouncing ball with his gloved hand. The loss to the Pine Knoll Knicks hurt every time he thought about it, which was at least several times a minute.

Of course it was worst whenever Rudy was around, smirking. At least there had been enough highlights during the game to provide ammunition for Ben to fight back. If Rudy talked about Austin's last shot, Ben reminded him that Austin had blocked one of Rudy's shots. But nothing could really erase the sting of defeat.

Every time the ball bounced off the side of the hoop or fell off the backboard, it sent a surge of anger through him. Each miss was a reminder of the shot he had missed near the end of the game. He was all through blaming Austin. "If I had made my last shot like I was supposed to, there wouldn't have been any lay-up for Austin to flub," he thought.

Mom opened the front door a crack and winced at the fury of the storm. "Benjamin, I'm worried about you!" she shouted. Ben could barely hear her, and the swirling snow made it just as difficult to see her. But it was not difficult to tell what was on her mind. Ken had already called him a certified looney for going out to play in a blizzard.

"I'll be coming in pretty soon," he shouted through his scarf. He doubted that she could hear that but it did not really matter. The door shut. Ben moved out toward the street, hunting for the free throw line. Already there was only a corner of blacktop near the garage that was still black. Ben had to scrape a line in the newly arrived snow where he thought the free throw line lay buried.

Even though the wind kept blowing his shots way off course, Ben refused to make any allowances for it. *There's no wind on a basketball court*, he thought. *I'll just practice shooting it up the way I'm supposed to and who cares if it goes in.*

Thanks to the wind, few of his shots did hit the basket. But Ben continued his practice until his eyes stung and his forehead throbbed from the force of the cold. *I hate those Knicks!* he thought as he brought the ball into the house and peeled the gloves off fingers that felt twice as thick as usual.

Coach Buckwell tried again to explain to Ben that basketball was not meant to be a one-man show. In fact, he used very close to the same words he had used the other night. But if those words had not been enough to convince Ben before the loss to the Knicks, they certainly carried no weight after it.

"I liked what you did the first few times down the court," Coach Buckwell said. Warm-ups had been delayed by the fact that 24 rows of chairs were sitting in the middle of Faith gymnasium. Several boys started removing the chairs while Ben's dad got a key to the storeroom. "When they double-teamed you, you immediately found Chris open."

"Yeah, and he just stood there with it," said Ben. As far as he was concerned, that was the end of the argument.

"He's not used to shooting," Coach said, rubbing one of his sleepy eyes. "You're in such control out there that some of those guys think they can't shoot without your permission. I guarantee you that if you keep finding the open man, pretty soon they'll know what to do with it. It may not pay off right away, but in the long run we'll be better off for it."

In the long run? thought Ben. *Who's he kidding? We only have five games left.*

The Faith gym was the smallest court in the league. Even though spectators pushed their folding chairs up against the wall, they still had to be careful that their toes did not touch or cross over the sideline.

Tonight's opponent was the Holy Family Flames. *We're the ones who should be called the Flames,* Ben thought, comparing the Falcons' bright red uniforms to the navy blue and gray of the Holy Family team.

Ben had been expecting a tough game. After all, the Flames had just beaten Pine Knoll to hand the Knicks their second loss. Greg Murphy had told him about one Flame player with thin, almost white hair who had muscles like a weight lifter. The guy was a tough, rough player who led the Flames to a four-point win.

Unable to see anyone on the court he would be afraid to arm wrestle. Ben asked one of the Flames about him.

"That's Jesse. He's got the flu," the boy said.

Ben smiled for the first time since the loss to the Knicks as he repeated the news to Rags and Pablo. "That makes our job easier," he said.

"You know what they say," Pablo nodded. "It's better to be lucky than good. If we beat them, we'll be 6-2, and in a four-way tie for first place."

"Who would have believed it?" marveled Rags.

"What do you mean 'who would have believed it'?" scolded Ben. "I expect to win every time we play."

"Yes, and I admire that," said Pablo, backing away from him. "No wonder Ms. Marinetti likes you so much!"

"Shut up!"

Coach Buckwell assembled his troops and read out the starting assignments in his usual monotone voice. "David and Ben at guards, John and Chris at forwards, Austin at center. Let's go!"

Ben was several steps onto the court before the last name sank in. "Did he say Austin?" he asked Rags. Sure enough, Pablo was shrugging at them from the bench while Austin was adjusting his socks and walking out with the rest of them.

Even with his size advantage, Austin barely won the opening tap. Ben scooped up the ball and cruised down the left side of the court. Only one player came out to challenge him; the rest had all paired up against the other Falcons. "That makes me the open man," he grinned to himself. He faked a pass, which got his opponent lunging for air.

"Shoot it, Ben!" said Donny, who was sitting with the other Falcons on the sidelines just a few feet away.

As Ben went up for the shot he heard Pablo answer, "You don't have to tell that to Ben. He'll pass up a shot about once every solar eclipse."

Although the shot went in, Ben did not get his usual stroke of pleasure from watching the net ripple. His own friend was talking about him as if he were a ball hog or something. *Coach wanted good shots, well, there it was,* he thought. *Couldn't have been easier if they had given me an escort to the basket.*

As he backpedaled down the court, he was so furious with Pablo that he forgot about the full court press. "Hey, Oak, get your buns back here!" yelled Rags, who had dogged one of the Flames only to see him bounce a pass to a completely unguarded teammate.

The close walls were awful. Ben could clearly hear some tittering among the parents at Rags's impolite comment. *Really funny,* he thought, angrily. *OK, everyone thinks I'm just a hotdog scorer? All right you guys, let's see who thinks they can shoot the ball!*

Holy Family missed their shot and Austin rebounded. Rags loped down court and automatically passed it to Ben. "Start cutting to the basket," Ben snapped at him. "Don't just stand there."

Rags did as he was told but the defenders had

heard the same message and knew what was coming. They closed in on Rags, cutting off the passing lane. "Don't just stand there," Ben waved at the others. "If someone wants the ball, you'd better move around."

He dribbled slowly as he stood about 20 feet from the basket, waiting for a teammate to break clear. He was not even paying any attention to the little Flame who had moved in to guard him more tightly. Once the guy even tipped the ball, but Ben recovered it. Of the four choices of targets, Austin seemed the best bet, so Ben whipped the ball to him, perhaps a little harder than he should have. Austin juggled the ball but came up with it. Then, taking a deep breath as if about to dive under water, the big center swung into a hook shot. The ball bounced off the front of the rim and the Flames rebounded it.

Ben gave him an almost fatherly smile before going back to work on defense. This time the Flames scored to even the game at 2-2. *Okay, who wants the ball this time?* Ben said to himself, again dribbling slowly, watching his teammates. The little Flames defender was growing more and more bold. Ben tried to ignore him but the guy would not quit. He kept sneaking in and getting a hand on the ball.

Growing irritated, Ben nearly shoved him with his forearm but checked himself in time. Again the guard ducked in and slapped at the ball. This time he ticked it enough so that it bounced off the side of Ben's leg and rolled out-of-bounds. Without thinking, Ben shoved the pesky opponent hard with the heel of his hand. "Get out of my face, shrimp!" he said.

A blast from a whistle pierced the gymnasium and a small man in a striped shirt ran towards Ben as if he were going to place him under arrest. "Technical foul!" he said. "Blue team shoots a free throw and then gets the ball out-of-bounds. If I see that again, son, you're out of the game."

Coach Buckwell beat the referee to it. He held a short conference with Pablo who ran in to take Ben's place. No one needed to tell Ben that he had just made a fool of himself. By the time he reached the row of folding chairs by the exits he was so frustrated and angry at everyone, including himself, that he wanted to cry. He headed for the last chair in the row but Coach Buckwell patted the empty chair next to him. Ben debated ignoring him, but something inside told him that he had already stirred up enough trouble for one day.

He slumped into the chair and stared at the floor. At the moment he did not have the slightest interest in the basketball game that was going on.

While keeping his eyes on the game, Coach Buckwell asked, "Do you know why you hit him?"

"No," said Ben, and at least for the moment, it was the truth.

"He made a good play on you," said the coach, still watching the game. "You weren't expecting that, were you?"

"No," Ben admitted.

"You didn't take him seriously enough. Then he embarrassed you by beating you, and you hit him. Maybe you should sit and think about that for a little while." The coach spoke without a trace of anger or any other kind of emotion. It suddenly flashed through Ben's mind what the Knicks' coach, Mr. Peters, would have done if he had been Ben's coach.

Ben sat silently, still feeling as though tears might come at any moment. *Fine, I'll think about it,* he thought. *That'll do a lot of good!* The "little while" that Coach Buckwell had spoken of turned out to be the entire game. As he realized he was not going to get back into the game, Ben felt more anger flowing into his already confused swirl of emotions. This was a game that they could have won easily if he had played.

But as it turned out, they won anyway. By playing forward instead of center, Pablo found it much easier to get off his shot, and he made the most of it. Austin figured out what to do with that extra length of bone that he had been blessed with. He blocked several shots, sank two out of five free throws, scored his first basket on a rebound shot, and even made one of those hook shots he had been practicing. This, along with the usual thievery from Rags and a few scattered points from the other players propelled the Falcons to a 27-22 win.

Rags and Pablo tried to console Ben, but there was not much they could say. Ben's dad surprised

93

him by putting a hand on his shoulder. *I'm surprised he'll admit that this little hothead is his son*, Ben thought. But Dad could not think of much to say, either. Ben's teammates were too thrilled over their own efforts to get bogged down in his gloom for more than a few seconds. Ben overhead more than one Falcon remarking, as if they still could not believe it, that they "had done it all without Ben."

Yeah, well, what if that Jesse character had shown up? Ben thought, as his giddy teammates congratulated each other. *Where would you be then?* The place suddenly felt hot and stuffy, and Ben wanted to get out as quickly as possible. Dad quietly nodded when Ben told him not to wait, that he needed to walk home alone.

It isn't fair, Ben thought as he sat in the hall to put on his boots. *I've always treated them well when I had a good game and everyone else messed up.* He could not begin to understand how he had gone from star of the team to a dirty player and a ball hog who hardly felt like part of the team at all. This was basketball; he was supposed to be having the best time of his life.

Something in the left boot was pinching his toe, and Ben absently pulled off the boot. Digging around for the problem, he discovered a familiar, crumpled object. It was square and very blue.

Not wanting anyone else to see it, he quickly slipped his foot back into the boot, put on his coat and hat, tucked his gloves in his armpits and stepped outside. He waited until he was under the first streetlight before taking out the envelope from his pocket. The paper was already cold and he hurriedly warmed his hands in his gloves before reading the note. This time the message was different and totally took him by surprise:

The Lord bless you and keep you,
The Lord make his face shine upon you.
The Lord lift up his countenance upon you and give you peace.
Order of the Broken Arrow

Ben had heard the words 100 times at least, in church. He had daydreamed through them, talked through them, and absently recited them. Now for the first time, these were words addressed only to him. They seemed to jump out at him from the page. The words were talking to him now—maybe they always had, but he had never heard them. At the moment it was hard to imagine that they had been written with anyone but him in mind. Ben was not sure exactly what they meant, but it was impossible to read them and still feel completely alone.

"Thanks, whoever you are," he said out loud to the mysterious sender of the note.

10
Night of Terror

Camp Drury was a 1,600-acre woodland playground filled with snow, deer, birds, and other creatures. There were two snow-covered lakes tucked back in the middle of the pine forest, one steep, open hillside on which a toboggan run had been built, and almost complete privacy for the scout troops who used it. These advantages more than made up for the crude indoor facilities. The concrete bunkhouse was equipped with a refrigerator, stove, sink, and a showerless bathroom. They did not make up for the fact that, for the first time in many months, Ben Oakland would not be within 20 miles of a basketball hoop.

It was a poor time for such a situation. The Falcons were now 8-2, still tied for first place, with only two games to go. The last thing Ben wanted to do was spend a weekend without any kind of practice.

Not that things were going particularly well for him on the court. Basketball was no longer the

96

simple game it had been at the start of the year. Now it seemed as though a panel of judges sat ready to rule on every shot he took. Ben had made a conscious effort to pass off whenever double-teamed. But now he sometimes felt guilty shooting even when he was wide open. Was it a "good" shot or a selfish one? Was someone going to gripe because their best shooter was still taking more shots than some of the others? Ben could hardly tell anymore.

Half of the group of 16 boys was perched atop the bunk beds that were scattered around the room. The rest had been nabbed for cleanup duty following a supper of barbecued beef sandwiches, carrots, and potato chips.

"Can we go exploring after we get these done, Mr. Barton?" asked Pablo, as he sloshed water in the large, battered pot that had held the barbecue.

The leader, a short, thick-bearded man with swatches of blond hair surrounding a bald spot, looked at his watch. "You've got free time until 9:30. Then we're going to roast some marshmallows outside and tell stories. I don't want you going too far off at night by yourselves, though. Where are you going?"

"We thought we'd try to find a toxic waste dump so we can get rid of the rest of the barbecue," Pablo said. Mr. Barton glared at him.

"Pablo and Ben and I just want to do down to the lake for a little while," Rags offered.

Although the weather was exceptionally mild this

evening, it had been bitterly cold for most of January. Ben knew that the ice would be solid well into spring. A trail led straight from the cabin to the lake a half mile away. Since they could not get lost or fall through the ice, there was no reason not to let them go.

Mr. Barton arrived at the same conclusion. "All right. Just stay together and don't do anything dumb. You got flashlights? And bring along a compass just in case."

Ben rolled his eyes at Rags on hearing the last comment. He wondered if Mr. Barton ever so much as went to the grocery store without a compass. Their departure was delayed when Mr. Barton inspected the pot and told Pablo to come back and do a better job of washing. But it was not long before Ben and his two friends stepped out into the night. They flicked on their flashlights but found that they really did not need them. A three-quarters moon was just about directly overhead and lighted up all but the densest portions of the woods. The air was so still that nothing could be heard but the crunching of their boots over the snow.

"I love the smell of pine," said Rags.

"Wooo, aren't we romantic?" teased Pablo.

"Hey, if you lived downwind from the paper mill like I do, you would appreciate what clean air was," said Rags.

"Do you realize that our last game against Brook Manor could be for the championship?" asked Ben.

"If we beat Meadow Hills and then Brook Manor beats Pine Knoll, we'll be the only two teams with a 9-2 record."

Rags and Pablo looked at each other. "The kid's talking basketball again," said Pablo. "Should we dump him in a snowbank?"

"Give him one more chance," said Rags.

Ben managed to stay off the subject as they wound down the trail to Crescent Lake. The moonlight that reflected off the white snow spread an amazing amount of light over the lake. Ben could clearly see the expressions on his two friends' faces.

"Look! Deer tracks!" shouted Rags, pointing to a cluster of prints that crossed the lake. "I wonder if they're still around."

"If they were, you just scared them off with that noise," scolded Ben. They followed the deer trail as it cut across the narrow section of the lake to where it led into the forest, but saw no sign of the animals.

"Whew! I'm hot!" Pablo said, unzipping his coat. "That was dumb of me to wear this sweatshirt underneath."

"I wonder if it's warm enough for snowballs," Ben said, dipping his gloves into the snow. Surprisingly, the snow held together.

"I suppose you're going to roll some basketball-sized snowballs and run us through a little passing drill," said Pablo.

"No, I'm going to make a baseball-sized one and rub it in your face," laughed Ben, charging. That set off a brief, three-sided snowball fight that was brought to an end by a chunk of snow that hit Pablo's neck and slid down his shirt. After that they began rolling snowballs.

"We're Troop 101," said Rags. "Why don't we make our sign right out in the middle of the lake? Pile up three snow balls for the ones and roll one gigantic ball in the middle for the zero."

The three worked hard at their project. By the time they shoved and strained at the last and largest of the snowballs, their necks were soaked with sweat. Just as they wheeled the five-foot diameter "zero" into place, Rags said, "Hey, we're not alone. See those lights over there? Over there," he pointed, "by the summer overnight camp."

Sure enough, at least four flashlight beams could be detected. Faint peals of laughter carried across the lake.

"I wonder who it is," said Ben. "Mr. Barton said there wasn't going to be anyone else up at Camp Drury this weekend."

"Must be our troop then," Pablo said. "I guess we weren't the only ones who wanted to go out for a walk."

"It's got to be the whole troop," said Rags. "They're building a fire. Looks like we're having the marshmallow roast down here."

"Come on," said Ben. "Why would they come all the way down here to build a fire? Especially without telling us?"

"They knew we were down here at the lake," Rags said. "It must be them! Who else could it be?" Their line of sight was blocked by pines and shrubs and the newly kindled fire was still too small to cast much light on any of the figures.

"Let's ambush them," Pablo whispered excitedly.

"How?" asked Rags. "We're standing out here in the middle of lake with the moon shining all over us. How can they miss us?"

"Just get off the lake and come around from the back side. We can spray them with smallbore snowball fire before they know we're there."

Rags and Ben agreed. They walked back towards the eastern shore, in no apparent hurry. As soon as they were off the lake, they plunged into the shadows. Pockets of deep snow, past their knees in spots, slowed their progress and it was not until fifteen minutes later that they began to approach the campfire from the wooded hill.

Ben found to his disgust that the snow was not as sticky in the more shadowed woods as it was out on the lake. He had to press hard with his soggy gloves to get it to hold together. "We'll have to carry one in each hand," he whispered. "We won't have time to make any once we start firing."

They slid and crawled down the hill, trying to keep from disturbing too many branches. Something did not seem quite right to Ben. He was not able to recognize for certain any of the laughs he was hearing. At last they reached the outhouse and found the snow more packed and easier to walk on. With Pablo in the lead, they crept forward to the last stand of scrub pine ringing the circle.

Peeking through white-dusted boughs, Ben saw a sight that froze his heart. His inner suspicions had been correct—it was not Troop 101!

Instead he saw five boys, probably high school aged. Their faces glowed in the yellow of the camp-fire and Ben did not like what he saw. Some of their eyes were glazed over, others looked as wild as those of a pony in a snake pit, and still others had that narrowed squint of plain meanness. There were beer cans lying around the edges of the circle and liquor bottles propped up next to the logs. One of the trespassers, dressed in baggy army fatigues and sporting a shaved head was swigging from his own bottle. A greasy-haired member of the gang was passing around a roach clip while another was snorting something out of his hand.

"Let's get out of here," mouthed Pablo, eyes shin-ing white in the semidarkness. As they crept back along the outhouse path, it seemed as though they were making ten times the noise they had made on their way to the campfire. Ben wanted to break into a run. He nearly tripped as he walked up Pablo's back.

They had nearly reached the outhouse and were about to head back into the deep snow when a crash right in front of them made them all jump right off the ground! The outhouse door opened and out staggered a boy in an open hunting jacket, flannel shirt, and blue jeans. As he saw them standing, frozen by fear, his nearly shut eyelids snapped open.

"Hey, looka we got here!" he roared drunkenly. In the distant, flickering light of the campfire, he looked like a maniac, leering at them with his mouth wide open and that crazed glint in his eye, with uncombed hair shooting out at all angles from his head. Just as Ben was about to make a dash for the deep woods, the guy seemed to guess his thoughts. "Uh-uh," he said, shaking his head. He withdrew his hand from his coat pocket and slowly aimed a gun right at Ben's eyes.

Ben could not even summon the strength to close his eyes, but stared straight ahead. His head was swimming. He tried to find some proof that this was a dream. Slowly the barrel of the gun moved and pointed at Rags, then at Pablo.

By then some of the others had arrived to see what the fuss was about. Laughter and a torrent of filthy language spilled out of their mouths.

"Hey, lookathat," spluttered the one with the shaved head. "One of em's godda shnowball. They were gonnatack ush."

Ben saw that his friends had had the good sense to drop their snowballs some time before. He opened his hand to let his drop but the evidence clung to his glove so stubbornly that he had to shake it off.

"Yeah, they were gonna ambush us," said another.

The long-haired one roared with laughter and said, "Big tough guys, huh? Look at the weapons these big guys carry. Snowballs!" He moved closer, his breath stinking. "Want to see a weapon, boy?" His tongue flopping out of his mouth, he held up a large hunting knife to the light. "Show 'em yours, Brodie."

"I already did," said the outhouse visitor, taking turns pointing his revolver at the three of them.

Ben was too scared to even think. His eyes were cemented to the small black cylinder that he realized might be the last thing he ever saw. These guys were out of their minds—so wasted they didn't know what they were doing. They could squeeze a trigger and wake up the next morning without a clue as to what they had done.

"What are you doin' here?" asked the one called Brodie, weaving toward them, sweeping the air with his gun. Neither Ben nor his friends said anything, nor did they dare look at each other. "You know what I ought to do?" Brodie said, his face twisted from the effort of his speech. "I ought to blow your brains out."

"Yeah, blow their brains out!" roared a voice from back at the campfire. All the others laughed.

"No, I godda a bedder idea,"said Brodie, spinning the chamber of his weapon. "Let's make 'em play roulette."

More roars of approval. "Just how lucky do you feel?" cackled the one with the shaved head.

Another belched after taking a long drink from his bottle. "Aw, let 'em go."

"Thad woun't be 'spitable," said Brodie, who was having trouble spinning the chamber. "Come on, be palsh!" he said, leaning close to Ben's cheek and lowering his voice to a whisper. "Wan get high, man? We're gonna. Ain't we, guys? Ain't we gonna?"

"No, thanks, we have to go," Pablo finally said in a shaky voice.

"Aw, come on!" He called them a long string of unprintable names, which the rest repeated. Pablo kept shaking his head. Ben could not keep his eyes off the gun. He winced every time Brodie's finger started tapping on the trigger.

The boy who had stayed at the campfire staggered through the screen of small pines and collapsed in the dirt near their feet. "Blow their brains out, blow their brains out," he muttered over and over before passing out.

The others thought his behavior extremely funny. "Bulldog's really gone, man!" laughed the long-haired one. "Out cold! Let's take him down to the water."

"Yeah, throw him in the water!" roared the shaved one.

As Ben gaped in disbelief, Brodie tucked his gun inside the waist of his pants and grabbed the unconscious boy by the foot. "Down to water!" he howled. The rest all tugged at various limbs. Some of them were pulling in different directions, so hard that the boy momentarily woke from his stupor to swear at them.

Ben perked up as he saw an escape route opening up in this nightmare. If only he could be sure if they were faking or not. Could anyone really be so stupid as to stand out in the snow and not remember the lake was frozen? If the drunken teenagers were that far gone, maybe there was a chance of escape.

Rags was thinking the same thing. He touched Ben's arm and nodded in the direction of the woods. Ben shook his head. He could still see the handle of the gun as Brodie and his laughing bunch of buddies dragged their load toward the lake.

"Back up slow," Ben whispered. Whatever they did, they did not want to attract attention and remind anyone of their presence. *Just keep quiet, and don't panic*, he thought. *And don't faint*, he added to himself, feeling his stomach walls cave in from the terror.

The first section of the short drop from the camp to the lake was steep. As soon as the first of the trespassers struck that, they toppled over each other. Brodie had to let go of one leg, and he fell backward, laughing all the while.

"Go!" whispered Rags and Ben at the same time. Not wanting to get bogged down in the deep snow and steep hills in back of the outhouse, they tore off down the main trail back towards the lodge. Rags was much faster than the others, and he was soon flying out in front. All three of them stumbled at one time or other on a hidden root or rock or dip in the road, but they were too frightened to allow themselves to fall.

Fighting for his balance after one such stumble, Ben kept seeing a vision of drug-soaked monsters chasing him. He kept listening for the sounds of gunfire, ready to flinch at the first shot. But whether their tormentors had forgotten about them or been too wasted to chase them, there were no shots, no pursuing footsteps, no voices except for several different octaves of faraway laughter.

Rags was far out in front now and not looking to see who was behind. Feeling quite sure that they were not being followed, Ben eased up and waited for Pablo. But the memory of that gun and those crazed eyes spurred him back to a full sprint before he could draw a full breath.

By the time Pablo and Ben reached the bunkhouse, Rags had already been there long enough to arouse some action. Mr. Barton was charging down the trail to help them, while two of the boys ran down the main road toward the caretaker's cabin.

Fourteen pairs of eyes were staring out the window of the locked lodge when the flashing lights arrived about 15 minutes later. Two squad cars pulled up next to the building. After speaking to Mr. Barton, one of them radioed for more help. It seemed like a long time later that five muttering, cursing boys marched clumsily up to the parking lot, sur-rounded by four uniformed guides. Several minutes after these five had been packed away in the squad cars, two other officers arrived, each with the arm of a very limp and unspeaking person draped over his shoulder.

The officers seemed to be in no urgent hurry, and so Ben assumed that no one had gotten hurt. As the piercing red and blue lights disappeared around the bend, Mr. Barton looked at his watch.

"Nearly 11 o'clock. Anyone still want to roast marshmallows and tell stories?"

They passed out marshmallows to the boys who ate them cold, straight from the bag, and curled up in their sleeping bags. But it was a long time before Ben fell asleep. It was not unusual for him to lie awake at night, but for the first time in many months, he was not thinking about basketball.

11
Grandpa

By the time Ben returned home, his memories of that night's events were diluted by many hours of snow soccer and tobogganing. As a result, he was able to tell the story to his parents and older brother calmly, as if describing a story he had heard from somewhere else.

Deep down, though, the events had upset his sense of security, and he didn't even squirm when Mom hugged him close. "It'll be a long time before you go on one of those trips again!" she declared, firmly. Even though he did not agree, Ben decided to save that argument, if it ever really came up, for a later time.

At dinner the next evening, Mom seemed unusually quiet. She didn't even get up to serve dessert. Kids always set the table, Dad put on the meal, Mom served the dessert—that was how life had gone for as long as he remembered. But this time she sat as if she simply did not have the energy to lift a piece of apple crisp onto a plate. Dad went over to the counter to do the honors.

"Who wants ice cream with theirs?" he asked. The question was scarcely out before it was answered with a chorus of "me."

"Me, too," Dad said. "Too bad we don't have any. Who wants a big piece?" Ben and Ken stared at him suspiciously this time. Only April and Nick piped up, echoing each other with their usual enthusiasm. "Okay, big pieces for April and Nick. Small ones for the rest," said Dad.

Ken and Ben started to complain but Dad ignored them and gave both a normal-sized piece. "If by some miracle you can't finish, will you give the rest to the boys?" he asked the younger ones. Both agreed, and Dad winked at the older boys. It was a pretty safe bet there would be leftovers from those two plates. Mom still said nothing, except a quiet "thank you" when Dad set her dessert in front of her.

"You look tired, Mom," Ken said. "You gettin' sick?"

Mom shook her head. She and Dad exchanged a look and then she said, "We got some bad news today." Ben put the spoonful of apple crisp back on his plate. Bad news had a way of ruining a good taste, so he would wait a bit for his dessert. "The nursing home called this morning," Dad continued. "Grampa's not doing so well. Mom has been there most of the day."

Not so well could mean a lot of things, Ben

110

thought. *Some of them pretty bad. What does she mean?*

April immediately had her thumb in her mouth and was climbing on Mom's lap. "Is he going to die?"

"No, no," comforted Mom. "But he's going to need quite a bit more care from now on. He's had another stroke and . . ." Her eyes grew misty.

"He'll have to be in a wheelchair from now on," Dad finished. "And he will need some help doing very ordinary things, like eating and getting dressed. I don't think he'll be able to visit us anymore."

Ben did not like the silence that followed. He waited for someone to break it. Ken finally did. It was one thing older brothers were good for. "We can still visit him, can't we?"

"Yes," Dad said. "In fact it would be a good idea. Mom said he's not complaining about anything, but she can tell it's not easy for him."

"He's always been able to take care of himself," Mom said. "He even mowed his own lawn up until two years ago."

"How old is Grandpa?" Nick asked.

"He's only 74," Dad said.

"When were you planning on going?" Ken asked. "I could go tomorrow or the next day, but I've got to study for that big biology test tomorrow. I suppose I could go tonight anyway," he shrugged.

"No, you take care of your schoolwork," said Mom. "You can go another time."

111

"I want to go visit our Grampa," said April, bouncing insistently on Mom's lap.

"Me, too," chimed in Nick.

"Nick, you were up *very* early this morning. You can't be out that late. And, April, you have school tomorrow morning."

"I hate school!" frowned April.

"Were you planning on going tonight?" Ben asked.

"I was going to go after I finish some papers I need to get in the mail," Dad said. "Is your homework done?"

"Don't have any," Ben said. As soon as the others were all excused from the table, Ben finally began digging into his apple crisp. Mom was still at the table, sipping on a cup of coffee. He saw more wrinkles and creases on her face than he had noticed before and he felt bad that they had not been getting along. Not that it was all his fault, of course.

"What was Grandpa like when he was young, Mom?" Ben asked.

"Don't talk with your mouth full," she said. "When he was young? Oh, he was always playing around, teasing like your dad. He used to love sports just like you do," she added, taking off her glasses and rubbing her eyes. "Mostly it was softball and tennis, and later on golf." She snorted a little laugh. "He used to play your sport, too, but that was before I came along. You should see some of his old high school yearbooks. I guess he was quite the player. I

112

seem to remember he won some honors. Most valuable something or other—I don't remember."

She looked at him over her cup of coffee. For a moment Ben saw that sparkle or something in her eyes that always made him feel good. "So maybe you come by your love for basketball honestly," she smiled.

Although he did not say anything, Ben was grateful for the remark. For a while he had come to believe that everyone else in the family considered basketball to be some sort of disease.

Ben had learned his lesson last time he was at the Silver Haven Home. Old people like it hot. Ben could be baking to death and still Grandpa would complain of a draft in the room. This time he came prepared, wearing only a T-shirt under his winter coat.

This evening they took the elevator to a part of the home Ben had never seen before. The employees at the Silver Haven Home seemed friendly as they bustled around, yet as soon as the elevator doors opened, Ben detected that unpleasant odor. Half a dozen or so people sat around in the lounge, shriveled into their wheelchairs. Some of them greeted Ben and his dad as they stepped out. Ben answered them more pleasantly than he would have answered most people. One woman sat muttering to herself. The only thing Ben could understand was that she constantly repeated the word "piano."

113

They crossed the lounge and began hunting for Room 334. Dad found the sign that indicated that rooms 318-338 were down the hallway to the right. The door was open. But through the doorway all they could see was the shape of some feet under blankets at the bottom of a bed.

Dad knocked on the open door. "Grandpa?"

After a few seconds a weak voice asked them to come in. Ben hoped that his face did not give away the dismay that he felt upon seeing Grandpa. He was even thinner than Ben remembered. One side of his face drooped as if the flesh were sliding off the bone, a silvery stubble of whiskers showed on his chin.

"Good to see you, Grandpa," Ben said, trying hard to be cheerful.

"Eh, who's that?" Grandpa's face looked like that of a small child suddenly realizing he was lost in the middle of a large fair.

"Ben!" Ben knew he had to speak loudly to Grandpa.

"Elmer, it's Tom Oakland," said Dad. "Audrey's husband. And this is our son, Ben."

"Oh, yeah," said Grandpa with a pained smile. "Thank you for coming. It's good to have visitors. What day is today?"

"It's Tuesday, Elmer," said Dad, loudly. "Tuesday, January 31st."

"What am I supposed to be doing?" Half his mouth did not move when he spoke, and this made him very difficult to understand.

114

"Nothing, Grandpa," Ben offered, as he moved to the opposite side of the bed from his dad. Dad indicated that he should pull up the chair near the wall. "You can just talk to us."

Ben sat there nervously for a minute. There didn't seem to be much to talk about. All he could think of was to ask how Grandpa was feeling, and that did not seem to be a subject worth exploring.

"How's the Chevy working?" Grandpa finally asked.

"It got us over here tonight," said Dad. "Starts even on the coldest mornings. I have to admit, you sure know how to pick cars! We haven't had a bit of trouble with it in six years."

More silence. Grandpa seemed to have great difficulty getting his breath. It was even harder for him to turn his head, so he only looked at Dad.

"You never told me you were such a good basketball player," Ben thought to say at last.

"Huh? What did I forget?" Grandpa asked, his face contorted as he tried to shape it into a questioning look.

"You didn't forget anything!" Ben said, even louder than before. "Mom told me tonight that you were a star basketball player in high school. You never told me about that." It was amazing to think that this aching, worn-out old body had once been able to dribble and jump on a basketball court.

"Oh, that was a long time ago. Long time."

"What position did you play?"

"Oh, a little guard, a little forward. I could play both, you know."

Ben hoped it was not just his imagination that Grandpa seemed to be perking up a little. Grandpa's breath still rasped, and many of his facial muscles were still frozen. But that anguished look seemed to have faded, and his mind seemed sharper.

"Were you a scorer or a rebounder or a playmaker, Grandpa?"

"Oh, I was a shooter," Grandpa smiled, and his chest rattled with kind of a cough, as if he were trying to laugh. "I admit I wasn't much else. All I really knew how to do was shoot."

"What was your best game?"

Grandpa sat silent for a long time. Ben was ready to give up on that question and ask another one. "24 points against Heartland, 1928. We won the game by two points in overtime," Grandpa said. With a great effort, aided by Dad, Grandpa turned his head toward Ben. The eyes that had looked bewildered and vacant now focused clearly on him. "Didn't you win a game in overtime a little while back?"

Ben sat closer to the bed and leaned one elbow on it. "Well, almost. It wasn't quite overtime but I made a shot with time running out that won the game. I didn't know you knew about that." Grandpa just looked at him for a while. "Got any advice for me, Grandpa?" Ben asked. "Our team might be playing for the championship in a couple nights. I

116

could really use some good pointers."

"Yes, I have one," he said, struggling to get his lips to form the sounds. "Two hands. You're always more accurate with two hands."

Dad grinned at Ben from across the bed and shook his head. Grandpa had always insisted that the prehistoric two-handed set shot was the best way to score from long range.

The old man's eyelids suddenly grew droopy and Ben cast a worried look at his dad. Dad stood up and bent over the bed. "He's just tired," he said. "I think our visit probably wore him out. Especially being so late in the evening."

The eyelids pulled open and stared at Ben. In a couple of seconds Ben saw a hint of recognigion. "I'm sorry, but I am tired," Grandpa said. "Could you read for me out of my Bible? It's the last thing I do before bed."

Dad found the book, a large-print version, open on the bedstand. Ben thought that Dad was going to read it, but Dad handed the open book across the bed to him.

"What do you want me to read?" Ben asked.

"The next chapter."

"The whole thing?"

"Yes."

It was the twelfth chapter of Luke. Ben glanced ahead to see how far he had to go and his heart sank when he saw that this chapter went on for 59 verses. He read about hypocrisy and sparrows and then came across a story that was at least partially familiar. "The land of a rich man brought forth plentifully," he started. Ben read how the rich man kept tearing down barns and building bigger ones to hold all the grain he was harvesting. Just when he was feeling wonderful and secure, wham! "This night your soul is required of you; and the things you have prepared, whose will they be?"

It gave him the creeps to read that verse: it brought back so vividly the memory of the campfire and the crazed teenagers and the dark barrel of the gun pointed at his head. Ben kept reading to the end of the chapter, but even as he did, he kept seeing the gun.

During the drive home Ben leaned against the cold vinyl of the car door. He tried to imagine Grandpa pumped back up with blood and muscle and energy, running around a basketball floor. But the image of Grandpa kept dissolving into a picture of Ben Oakland on the court. Pretty soon the picture reversed itself and he imagined himself, 65 years from now, lying in a bed, trapped in a body that no longer worked. Trapped in a body that couldn't play basketball. Shoot, it wouldn't take 65 years—Grandpa had not been able to play real basketball for years, decades. Here was a man who had been a star player, and what did it mean now?

Boy, it all goes away so quickly, he thought. *It was a good thing basketball wasn't Grandpa's whole life.*

"This night your soul is required of you and the things you have prepared, whose will they be now?"

What would happen if I went tonight? Ben thought. It was a scary thought, but one that he couldn't help thinking. In fact, he had been forced to think it dozens of times since that night with the gun. How could he help but think of it?

Well, what would I have to show for myself besides basketball? he thought. *Nothing. Basketball's my life.* He had said those last three words many times before, only before he had been rather proud of himself. It did not sound very smart right now. *I can never get enough of basketball.*

"This night your soul is required of you; and the things you have prepared, whose will they be?" The phrase would not go away.

I never could get enough basketball, he admitted. *I can't help myself. I can't get enough points, enough wins. Tear down old barns, get new ones. More, more. Then it goes and what are you left with? Parents you can't get along with. Refs who think you're a crybaby. Teammates who think you're a ball hog. Opponents who think you're a poor sport.*

What else do I have?

12
Brook Manor Mavericks

The eleventh round of games on the schedule went exactly as Ben hoped it would. The Falcons boosted their record to 9-2, thanks to a 36-20 win over Sun Creek. Brook Manor then knocked Pine Knoll out of a first place tie with a 50-45 victory over the Knicks. That left the Brook Manor Mavericks tied for the top spot with Faith going into their final game showdown. One of them would be the champion.

"Could you stop drumming your knees?" Mom said to Ben as Dad pulled into the parking lot. "You're shaking the whole seat."

"I can't help it, I'm nervous," Ben said. He had found that after such a long period of not really speaking to his parents, it was not such a cinch to reopen communication. But at least he did not feel like he had to avoid his family anymore.

Brook Manor was the oldest elementary school still in use in the metro area, and the largest. The bricks had turned nearly black with age, and there weren't many growing things on the property even when the winter snows left. It was close to the business section, bounded on one side by an auto repair shop, and by a railroad track cordoned off by a chain link fence on the other. Behind the school stood a row of houses, and in front of it ran a main street carrying traffic into downtown.

"Are you going to win?" April asked as they piled out of the car.

"If I knew the answer to that we could have stayed home tonight," Ben said, speaking more loudly to be heard over the traffic. He took a deep breath. "Gotta keep control," he kept reminding himself. "It's just a game. All right, it's the most important game you've ever played in, but it's still a game."

There was a surprise waiting for Ben when he walked into the gym. Hanging across the entire length of one of the purple walls was a giant banner that read: "FIRE UP, FAITH FALCONS!" At the end of the fancy lettering was a lifelike picture of a red falcon soaring across a mountainside.

"Wow!" said Ken. "I thought you guys were the visiting team tonight! Looks like you own the whole gym. I've never even seen a sign like that at any of the *high school* games. I suppose next you'll be telling me you have cheerleaders."

"Yep. And television time-outs, too," nodded Ben. "But really, who do you think did that?"

"Almost looks professional," said Mom.

"Did you hear that?" Pablo said to Rags as they trotted over to greet the Oaklands. "Mrs. Oakland says it was done by a professional. That means Austin can't play on our team. We're not supposed to use professionals."

"Austin did that?" exclaimed Ben. "That's right, he told me he was an artist."

"He didn't lie," said Dad.

Ben tossed his jacket into a corner and ran out to where Austin had just begun to take some practice shots. "You mean to tell me this is what you were doing when you could have been practicing basketball?" Ben scoffed, surveying the mural. Austin stopped in his tracks. His shoulders slumped in a look of guilt and disappointment.

"Sure wish I could draw like that!" Ben added with a grin.

Austin broke into a relieved smile. "I wish I could play basketball like you."

"Well, if we ever find a genie and a magic lamp, I guess we'll know what to wish for."

Players from both teams trickled into the gym until at last two full teams were shooting at baskets on opposite ends of the court. Many of the players spent as much time sizing up the opposition as they did warming up. Each practice shot was examined as an omen of what was to come. Whenever a purple-shirted Brook Manor player missed a shot, the Falcons' hopes would rise. With each shot their opponents made, the Falcons' confidence would drop.

Pablo had seen enough to draw his own conclusions. "Looks like we're in trouble, Oak."

"That's a great attitude, Pablo," said Ben, who was practicing free throws and ignoring the Mavericks. "What makes you say that?"

"Are you blind? Look at them shoot!"

"Yeah? What about it?" Ben swished his third shot in a row.

Pablo was so concerned about the situation that he had not taken a shot for several minutes.

"Look," said Ben, putting a hand on Pablo's shoulder. "I know they've got a guy named Tyrone who's as good as anyone we've played. I remember him from a summer basketball clinic. But I don't know anything about the rest." He leaned close to Pablo's ear and cast some secretive glances left and right. "You know what Brook Manor is saying right now? They're looking over here and saying, 'Oh, no! They got a little guy who's going to run the pants off us. And look at that giant they've got playing center! We'll never get a shot off! And there's Ben Oakland, the guy who smacks you if you play him too close. Shoot, we might as well go home and mail in the score!"

Ben turned and sank another free throw. "And they're probably worried sick about that number eight who is so good he doesn't even have to warm up," he added. It took a couple seconds for that to sink in before Pablo called him a turkey and started shooting baskets.

Ben could hardly wait for Coach Buckwell's words of wisdom before the start of the game. This was for the championship, after all. The coach had to at least *try* to say something inspirational.

"Okay, listen up, guys," said the coach to nine players who had been waiting for him in silence for at least half a minute. "We're going to have to use the press. Play as hard as you can, and I'll keep substituting to keep you all fresh. David and Ben start at guard, Paul at center, Chris and Donny at forward." With that he rubbed his pocked cheeks and sat back in his chair.

Somehow it seemed comforting to hear Coach say the expected words. He might not know as much about the game as some other coaches, and he might not be much for pep talks. But he was always there for you, and he was fair. You had to give him that.

"Nice to know some things never change," Ben said to Rags as the two trotted onto the court. "Same speech for the 12th straight time."

"Except for the lineup," said Rags. "Why is he starting Donny?"

Coach's speech had started out so familiar that Ben had not listened to the end. "Really? Donny's starting?" He looked around and saw Pablo standing in the purple circle at center court. "And Austin's on the bench? He's been playing pretty well lately. Maybe Coach plans to substitute often and doesn't want all the best players on the court at once."

Tyrone walked over to Ben. Neither of them

124

offered their hands but Tyrone said, "How you doin'?" as they positioned themselves for the jump.

"I'd probably be doing better if you weren't guarding me," answered Ben.

"Just don't even be thinking about driving on me and we'll get along all right," smiled Tyrone.

"I like to live dangerously," said Ben. That brought a chuckle from Tyrone.

The Brook Manor Mavericks easily won the tap and raced downcourt before the Falcon defense could get organized. A couple of quick passes later, Tyrone banked in a short shot. Ben could have kicked himself. He had been unable to fight through the traffic, so Tyrone had been left all alone.

Rags ran the ball upcourt. Immediately after crossing the center line, he tossed the ball to Ben on the left side. Ben turned and found Tyrone crouched in front of him, one hand outstretched. Relaxing his muscles, Ben started to toss it back to Rags. Just before the ball left his hands, though, he pulled it back and burst past Tyrone. The Mavericks were prepared. One of the forwards stepped in to block his path. It was all quite familiar by now. Immediately Ben slid a pass to Chris who was standing unguarded at the side of the basket.

By the time Ben had opened his mouth to yell "Shoot!" Chris had already arched the ball into the air. It dropped through cleanly to tie the score. "Nice shot!" grinned Ben, slapping Chris's open palm.

"Nice pass," Chris beamed.

"Anyone feel like playing defense?" shouted Rags. Three purple-clad Mavericks were having no trouble playing keepaway from the lone Falcon defender in the backcourt.

"Sorry," said Ben, rushing up to reinforce him. But it was already too late. The Mavericks were rushing the ball towards the basket. Again they were able to get a shot from close range and, although it missed, they put in the rebound. "Get in the game, Oakland!" Ben said to himself angrily.

On offense, Ben repeated the same move he had tried last time, but Tyrone was already wise to him. Ben had to back out and give up the ball to Rags. Rags passed to Donny, who seemed happy just to have a chance to handle the ball. Donny passed to Pablo who backed in and looked for a shot. He tried to force it through the taller Mavericks and missed badly. But he was fouled on the play. He made the first foul shot and missed the second, leaving the Falcons one point behind.

This time the Falcons unleashed their full court press. The Mavericks had obviously prepared for it. Both of their forwards hovered near midcourt to help out in case the guards got trapped. But there was no way to prepare for Rags's quick, windmilling hands. He picked the guard clean and coasted in for a lay-up to put the Falcons into the lead.

After that, Tyrone took over most of the ball handling for the Mavericks. Ben was happy to see it.

126

Although the Falcons might not be able to get as many steals as usual, Rags's hounding defense and the double-team traps set by the other Falcons would take a lot out of the Mavericks' star. As a result, he might not have as much energy left for scoring and defensive work.

Unfortunately, there were other Mavericks who could score, even if Tyrone ever did show signs of tiring. They scored three straight baskets, two from in close and one from long range, while the Falcons could do nothing.

Into the game came Austin and John, out went Pablo and Donny. Austin's height had an immediate effect on the Mavericks' inside game. After Austin blocked the first shot taken against him, Brook Manor started thinking twice before shooting from in close. It did not seem to matter, though, because the smaller of the Mavericks' guards got hot from the outside. After the guard popped in two long-range shots, a weary Rags was taken out for a rest in favor of Nathan.

With the score now 14-5 in favor of Brook Manor, Ben began to tighten up. This was the title match. All that buildup, all those days and nights of thinking about it and preparing, and here the game was getting away from them even before the first quarter was over. With his jaw clenched he took the ball into the lane. As usual, Tyrone stayed right with him. This time Ben made his move toward the basket and fired. Swish! The score stood 14-7 as the whistle sounded ending the first quarter.

With Rags out of the game, the Falcon press was not nearly as effective in the next period. Tyrone galloped across the center line and sped for the hoop where Austin stood ready to challenge him. As Austin stretched out to challenge the shot, Tyrone slipped the ball to a teammate coming in from the other side. The Maverick cut in behind Austin for an easy basket to make it 16-7.

Ben took the ball as it fell through the net and slammed it on the floor before putting it back in play. Again he tried to work around his defender, and could not do it. He was forced to toss up an awkward shot that somehow went in. Sixteen to nine.

Tyrone answered with an almost identical shot, forced by Ben's tough defense. Ben ground his teeth. He was playing his heart out and somehow could not cut the gap.

Tyrone played him even closer this time down the court. *That means I should be able to drive around him*, Ben thought. He tried once, twice, and finally slid around his opponent's shoulder. Immediately two Mavericks stepped in to plug the middle. Ben kept going and launched a shot just as he crashed into one of them. The ball bounced off the glass into the hoop.

A shrill whistle echoed off throughout the gym. The referee put one hand behind his head, signaling a charging foul on Ben. "No basket!" he said, as he pointed toward the basket that the Falcons were defending. "Purple ball."

Ben bounced to his feet, so angry the veins ere bulging in his neck. With his arms clenched at his side, he ran at the referee, "He didn't have position!" he shrieked.

The referee stared at him coldly. His hands seemed to be twitching slightly. As Ben stared in anguish, he saw those hands begin to form a "t" signaling a technical foul on Ben.

13

The Last Shot

Before the referee could complete his sign, Ben beat him to it with a "t" of his own. "Time out!" he said, clapping the flat of one hand against the upraised fingers of the other.

The referee hesitated a second, then blew his whistle. "Time out, red team," he said.

"Whew!" thought Ben as he walked back toward the Falcon chairs with his head down. He exhaled deeply a few times to try and let out some of the frustration, then dropped heavily into the chair next to Coach Buckwell.

"You got to take me out," he said, resting his eyes in the palms of his hands.

Coach Buckwell had nothing to say during the time-out other than "good job" and "Paul, go in for Ben." It was not until the referee had resumed play that he spoke to Ben. "What's the problem? You hurt yourself?"

Ben pulled his hands away from his eyes and waited for his vision to clear itself of those swirling colors. "I'm not hurt. I just lost control," he said bitterly. "I was trying, I was really trying, but I can't do it. I just can't stand losing! I started acting like an idiot again. I don't know why I do that!"

Coach Buckwell slowly scratched an itch on his leg. "That was my fault, Ben. It's a coach's job to get a player off the floor when he starts to get that way. You showed a lot of class taking yourself out."

Ben accepted the praise silently. He wanted to believe what his coach was saying but there were too many facts in the way. He had come into the game with what he had thought was a new attitude, only to find that he had not changed much at all. The only new thing was that now he was able to recognize when he was acting like a fool.

"We'll get you back in there in the second half," said the coach. "For now, just sit back and close your eyes. Oh, and someone asked me to give you this."

His thick, hairy hands were holding out a blue envelope. "Who gave you this?" Ben said, sitting upright.

"Someone," said the coach, turning his attention back to the game.

Ben turned the envelope over in his hand for a few seconds. Should he be reading this in the middle of a game or should he wait? Curiosity won out and he tore open the top. This time the letter was not written in that juvenile script but in flowing, adult handwriting:

131

"Ben,

However the game turns out, you have a right to be proud. It's a blessing to see the effort you put out. You and all the Falcons have been a joy to watch.

Order of the Broken Arrow

P.S. The ref blew the charging call!"

Ben whirled around. The letter writer had to be in the gym at this moment! Frantically he searched the spectators' faces for some give-away clues. But all he saw were parents earnestly watching the game, some younger children paying far less attention, and a custodian who passed through the gym, looking at his watch. No one was giving away anything.

"What are you looking for, Ben?" asked April, sitting in a row of chairs directly behind him.

"Nothing," he said, and he began to turn around. Suddenly an idea struck him. "April, come here." She bounded off her chair eagerly, pigtails flopping. "April," he whispered, "did you see anyone give my coach a blue envelope?"

April's lips snapped shut as tightly as if someone were trying to force a spoonful of spinach down her. Her shoulders stiffened as she shook her head quickly and scurried back to her chair. "That little squirt knows and she's not telling," he thought. But there was someone else there who could not keep a secret for anything. "Nick, come here," Ben beckoned.

Nick hopped down from his chair in a perfect imitation of April. "Nick, old buddy, this is really

132

important. Did you see anyone give a blue envelope to this man sitting next to me?"

You would have thought he had threatened Nick's life. The kid stood almost paralyzed, looked pleadingly at Mom and Dad, and then shook his head. The answer to the mystery was just beginning to dawn on Ben when he saw the buttons. Both Mom and Dad were wearing small black buttons on which was drawn a white arrow with the shaft broken. Order of the Broken Arrow. That's who had been sending those notes all along! How could he have been so dumb?

Ben pushed through the Falcons' row of seats and kneeled between his parents. "I should have known it was you," he said.

"We didn't tell," insisted April.

"Why should you have known?" asked Dad.

"I don't know, I just should have," said Ben. "Thanks. There were some times when the notes really came in handy." This was getting to be a humbling night in many ways.

"Our pleasure," said Dad.

Then, whispering so she wouldn't disturb those around watching the game, Mom said, "You know we weren't communicating very well for a time. It just seemed like things had gotten so bad between us that we couldn't talk to each other. So if we can't talk, how do we let you know we really care about you? We hoped this might help break the ice."

"Maybe we won't be needing to use notes

anymore?" Dad suggested hopefully.

"Maybe not," Ben said. "So tell me, was it April who printed all those notes for you?"

"Excellent deduction, Sherlock," said Dad. "It was good penmanship practice for her."

"And what is the Order of the Broken Arrow?"

"Broken arrow—no more war?" said Mom.

Ben nodded. "Well, I'm sorry to have to say this, but you're both dead wrong about one thing."

"What's that?" said both parents suspiciously.

"The ref was right. I charged."

By the time he got back to his seat next to Coach Buckwell, the half was nearly over. Ben could not believe he had totally ignored nearly a quarter of play in a championship game. Fearful of what he would see, he checked the portable score board perched on the scorer's table. Incredibly, the Faith Falcons had closed the gap to 24-22.

"How did that happen?" Ben asked Rags as the Falcons walked off the court at halftime.

"Who knows?" smiled Rags.

"No, I mean how?" Ben said. "I didn't see what happened after I left. Who scored for us and what happened to Tyrone?"

Rags couldn't help laughing. "Are you serious? You didn't watch any of it? What's the matter, did the game get too boring for you?"

"Would you just tell me?"

"Sure," Rags shrugged. "As soon as you left the game, Tyrone sat down, too. He was pretty tired and they must have figured that with you out they could afford to give him a rest. After that they started to have trouble against our press. Austin blocked another shot and scored a basket on that miserable excuse for a hook shot you taught him. The rest was just like the last couple of games. With Austin drawing attention near the basket, Pablo had room to shoot and he hit a few of them. John got a basket after a rebound and I made a couple of free throws and here we are!"

"Listen up, boys," Coach Buckwell called. Ben could not help but think it was probably the last time he would ever hear that familiar call. He would miss it. It wasn't just the game of basketball he would miss; it was all these guys playing together. Maybe that was the mark of a good coach. "They've been getting a number of baskets from that guard, number 16," he said, consulting his notes. "Don't worry about that. If he can keep making those from out there, then they deserve to win. I'd be surprised if he does. Keep the press going hard. We'll keep substituting to keep fresh. And, Austin, when you're in the game, give Ben some help with that number 5. He's dangerous."

"He crossed us up," grinned Rags as they took their positions on the court. "Added a new wrinkle to the standard speech."

Ben had been sitting so long that the drafty gymnasium air had chilled his once sweaty body. He wished he could have shot a few baskets before getting back into action. As he performed a few hops and short sprints to loosen up, he saw Tyrone coming toward him.

"You okay, man?" Tyrone asked.

"Never better," Ben answered. "And you? How's the wife and kids?"

Tyrone laughed and then broke some welcome news to him. "Coach wants me to concentrate on bringing up the ball and scoring. He doesn't want me wearing myself out trying to chase your hide all around the court. So you're safe; someone else will be guarding you from now on."

"Wish I could say the same for you," Ben answered. "I still got you. Just don't be trying to drive on me and you'll be all right."

"I like to live dangerously," said Tyrone.

In getting rid of Tyrone, Ben felt as though he had been released from a straitjacket. He repeatedly drove into the lane for lay-ups or else passed off to an open Falcon for an easy shot.

Tyrone was equal to the challenge, however. Now that he had gotten used to the Falcons' full court press, he cut through it easily. Although Ben made him work for everything he got and forced him to take some off-balance shots, the Maverick star kept scoring. Austin's shot-blocking had intimidated a couple of the other Mavericks, but he could not seem to get a hand on anything Tyrone tossed up. Worse yet, Austin was constantly being pushed out of position for rebounds. One of the

Brook Manor forwards scored an easy rebound basket to push his team ahead 38-37 at the end of the third quarter.

Austin trudged wearily to the last chair in the row, where he would be sitting at the start of the final period. Ben followed him to give him some encouragement. "You know, Austin, you're doing a lot of things right. You just need to be more aggressive. You're being too gentle out there. Do you realize you haven't been called for one foul all year long?"

Austin rubbed a bead of sweat off the end of his large nose. "You're right!" he marveled. "I haven't committed a single foul, have I?"

In the final quarter, Ben scored two more baskets before sitting down for a rest. He expected to see Rags hop off his seat to take his place but instead the coach sent Donny.

"Why didn't you sent Rags in, Coach?" Ben asked.

Coach Buckwell waited so long to answer that Ben was not sure he had been heard. "We'll turn Rags loose with fresh legs the last two minutes. He should be able to make something happen."

Meanwhile Tyrone was still making things happen for Brook Manor. Just as Coach Buckwell had predicted, the Mavericks' other guard started missing his shots. But Tyrone had twice muscled his way into the middle to pull down rebounds. Now that Austin was out of the game, the Brook Manor center also started to take the ball to the hoop. He scored twice against Pablo to put his team ahead by four, 45-41.

"Ben, Austin in. Donny, Paul out," Coach Buckwell said. Although many in the crowd were beginning to squirm from the mounting pressure, the coach showed no emotion, as usual.

Ben scored on a drive to the basket. Tyrone answered with a high-arching shot from beyond the free throw line. The Falcons were still four points behind. The clock showed 3:42 to play.

As Ben dribbled downcourt, debating his next move, a familiar face came up to challenge him. Tyrone winked and inched closer, ready to pounce the instant Ben made a move. The move caught Ben by surprise. He checked his teammates and his gaze lingered on Austin, who had his arms stretched out, begging for the ball. Austin's powers of persuasion worked, because Ben found himself lobbing a pass to him. The tall center bobbled the ball, then took a long awkward step and swung his arm around. The hook shot rolled around the rim twice before dropping through.

"Two points behind," thought Ben, "We've got to stop them here."

Ben clung to Tyrone like a tight-fitting jacket and the Brook Manor star was finally forced to give up the ball to a teammate. A shot went up and bounded high off the rim. As he outfought a Maverick forward for the ball, Ben caught a glimpse of disaster out of the corner of his eye. There was Austin pushing the Maverick center, as plain as if they were two kids fighting over a toy. A whistle blew; the foul was called. Instead of it being the Falcons' ball, Brook Manor had a chance to add to their lead at the free throw line. Yet there stood Austin looking quite satisfied with himself.

"What do you think you're doing?" challenged Ben, feeling his frustrations slipping out of control again.

"I fouled him," Austin said, innocently. "You said I was supposed to be more aggressive, didn't you?"

Ben stared stupidly at Austin for several moments. "Look," he said, trying hard not to laugh at Austin's ignorance. "Never mind what I told you. No more fouling, okay?"

As the Maverick center stepped to the line, Rags dashed into the game for John. "Two-minute warning," Rags said, grimly. Ben looked over at Tyrone, who had his hands on his knees and was breathing heavily. He could not help thinking that Coach Buckwell was right. A fresh Rags romping among tired bodies with two minutes left in a championship game could create some problems for the Mavericks.

The center made his first shot and missed the second. Brook Manor now led, 48-45. Again Tyrone was all over Ben. Ben passed to Austin who was called for traveling. Before Ben had time to be disappointed, there was Rags bouncing along the end line, ready to deny the inbounds pass. The other

Falcons joined the attack. Tyrone could not get open for the pass. Instead the throw went to another Maverick who dribbled the ball off his knee.

Ben and two Mavericks chased the ball from different directions. Ben got there first, just before an on-rushing Maverick who knocked him to the ground. Foul.

"You okay?" Rags asked him.

Ben nodded and accepted his friend's offer of an outstretched arm. After shaking his head to clear the fuzziness, he sank both free throws to pull Faith within one point.

Brook Manor tried a dangerous inbounds pass to Tyrone, who had to outleap Chris and Ben for the ball. He fought his way past Rags and into the front court. Gulping air, Ben moved over to challenge Tyrone. Less than a minute remained. This was a defensive play he just *had* to make.

"David!" shouted Coach Buckwell. "Switch with Ben!"

Quickly Rags cut in front of Ben and started waving his hands all over Tyrone. Ben felt hurt at first that he had been taken off the Maverick star, but it took him only a couple seconds to appreciate the move. Rags was fresh. Short, but fresh and as pesky a defender as there was. Tyrone tried to move in, thought better of it, and passed in to the center. Feeling Austin's shadow over him, the center immediately fired it back to Tyrone.

This time the Brook Manor star backed Rags in

toward the basket. Closer and closer he got, while Rags fought him tenaciously for every inch. Finally Tyrone turned around and jumped. Rags was far too short to challenge the shot but Austin had somehow guessed what was coming. As the ball left Tyrone's hand, Austin's bony fingers rose just high enough to tip it off course. John grabbed the rebound and flipped it to Rags who sped down the court at top speed.

Unable to set up their defense, Brook Manor had lost track of Ben. Rags was the first to spot him cutting under the basket. His pass was so hard it stung Ben's hands and he nearly lost it out-of-bounds. But he recovered, and stepped back to put in the lay-up. The Falcons were ahead!

This time Ben's mind was totally on the game. "Press!" he shouted. He stood by the end line to deny the pass while Rags became Tyrone's second layer of clothing. Suddenly the passer's eyes grew huge. He reared back like a football quarterback and threw as hard as he could. Ben whirled around to see what was happening.

Apparently the pace had been too much for Austin who stood gasping for air in the Mavericks' backcourt. His absence had left the Maverick center all alone under the other basket! Rags had seen the danger, too. He had left Tyrone and started streaking down the court a second or two before the pass was made.

The ball was traveling so high and fast that the

141

Maverick had to first knock it down with his hand, then catch up with it. This delay was just enough for Rags to arrive on the scene. The Maverick took two dribbles towards the basket. As the ball hit the ground for the last time before he jumped into his lay-up, Rags slapped the ball backwards towards center court.

Bodies were spread all over the court by this time. Chris reached the ball first near the half court line and threw it to Ben who had hardly moved from under the basket.

"This will clinch it!" he thought as he turned toward the basket. There was no Maverick within 20 feet of him. Such a surge of energy flowed through him that he could almost imagine dunking the ball. But before he laid the ball up, he saw Austin trotting in.

Without quite thinking why, Ben stopped and flipped the ball to Austin. "It's all yours," he said. Austin cradled the ball in one huge hand and took two choppy steps. As Ben gaped in horror, Austin missed! Tyrone roared in to take the rebound. Dribbling madly back the other way, the Maverick looked feverishly at the scoreboard and saw "01." Gathering all his strength, he unleashed a shot from near center court.

The ball seemed to hang in the air for several seconds, aiming straight for the Mavericks' basket. But it just missed, banging the front rim so hard that the entire backboard shook.

The Falcons dashed around the court trying to find each other so they could share their celebration. Amid the madness, Ben saw his parents hoist April and Nick high in the air and twirl them around. The only sane Falcon backer seemed to be Coach Buckwell, who was calmly walking over to shake hands with the Maverick coach. The last thought that occurred to Ben was that he was glad it was Coach Buckwell taking that little walk instead of, well, instead of anyone else.

When the chaos finally settled, Austin sheepishly stuck out a hand to Ben. "I don't know if I have the nerves for this sport," he said. "Art is much more peaceful. You know, I appreciated the thought. But you should have taken that last shot yourself."

Ben grabbed his hand and slapped him as high up his shoulder as he could reach. "Maybe," he grinned, as April and Nick charged full speed into him from across the floor. "But somehow I don't think Coach minded. Hey, it's like any gift—it's the thought that counts."